He Sai...

She Said

She

To my beloved Eric for believing in me;
to my treasure Diana for making me laugh;
and to my faith big brother Todd
for kicking me in the skirt to write.

He

To Michelle, Eric, & Diana

He Said . . .

She Said

Biblical Stories from a Male and Female Perspective

Michelle Kallock Knight
and Todd Outcalt

CHALICE
PRESS

ST. LOUIS, MISSOURI

Cover and interior design: Scribe Inc.

www.chalicepress.com

10 9 8 7 6 5 4 3 2 1   12   13   14   15   16   17

PRINT: 9780827214866   EPUB: 9780827214873   EPDF: 9780827214880

Library of Congress Cataloging-in-Publication Data
available upon request

Printed in the United States of America

Contents

Chapter 1

Abraham and Sarah

Genesis 15—24

In Genesis we discover how God chose to be connected to a particular people. God chooses Abraham and Sarah, not because they are perfect, but because they are faithful servants, willing to migrate to a new land. God offers this couple a star-filled sky of descendants and a land of their own in return for this covenant obedience.

God's call beckoned Abraham and Sarah to leave behind the city of Ur—an ancient city located on the Euphrates River (Iraq)—and travel to Canaan (Israel), a marginal land located along the Mediterranean Sea. Through Abraham and Sarah we get a glimpse of this ancient world of nomadic herdsmen, tribal alliances, polygamous marriages, and child sacrifice.

The story of Abraham and Sarah is our family story—a story shared by Jews, Christians, and Muslims. Each of these monotheistic faiths traces its genealogy and history back to this couple. The large themes in their story—who they were, how God related to them, and the promises God made long ago—remain as important and significant today as they were in the Middle Bronze Age (2200–1550 B.C.E.) in which they lived.

Welcome to our family history!

 # She Said

Now Sarai, Abram's wife, had borne him no children.
—Genesis 16:1a (NIV)

Reading the story of Abraham and Sarah's infertility brings out my deep compassion for these lonely parents-to-be. How ironic that a very private issue such as sexuality and fertility has become public theological discourse for centuries and is the "birthing" point of three major world religions! Sadly, I know too many couples within my family and church community who have struggled with infertility, premature births, death of their infants and toddlers, costly fertility treatments, or the long process of waiting to adopt a child.

The inability to conceive a child—for women and men—can feel like a deeply personal failure. A sperm and an egg are, after all, very personal things. These smallest of cells carry the deepest, most secret parts of our genetic code. Inability to conceive impacts a person's sense of womanhood or manhood and can therefore influence a person's identity, strength, virility, and vitality. Multiply our contemporary sensibilities on this subject a thousandfold for Sarah and Abraham, because they lived in the era when a woman was *only* worth something if she produced a male heir for her man. *Ouch. Poor Sarah.*

Her man wasn't just your average nomadic herdsman in the community—he was a businessman and a leader. People looked to Abraham *and* his wealth and therefore, by association, looked to Sarah for leadership as well. I wonder: Did Sarah have a diminished self-worth? Did she have the support of her loyal husband or draw stamina from her women friends? The way she held her head up amid the whispers of other folks is amazing!

Abraham never leaves Sarah. He could have dumped her for a newer, younger model of femininity and fertility. After all, in those ancient times the blame for infertility rested on the woman. Still Abraham keeps Sarah, and together they wait and wade through the promises of God even with the reality of infertility.

A present-day story might help: a wife begged her spouse to stop having sexual intercourse with her at a decisive point in their marriage.

Her reason? Not what you might think. This dedicated wife and mother was bone-tired and heart-weary of burying their dead babies. Only two of her many pregnancies ever made it to live births. Thus she hoped to avoid any more sorrow by not participating in the act of procreation. She was like an old-school Catholic lady in her upbringing, taught by her church that any form of birth control was not an option. How sad! This issue finally tore this couple apart and led to their divorce.

The immense grief of losing a child is a difficult hurdle for any parent. I weep with Sarah in her struggle and in her silent losses, because scripture says she is barren and thus cannot become pregnant nor bear a child (Gen. 11:30). Abraham's generation considered this condition "a curse or affliction sent by God (Gen. 20:18), primarily because procreation was considered to be both a commandment and a blessing (Gen. 1:28; 9:7; Ps. 127:3–5).

As a mother I, too, suffered through pregnancy loss. The pain and disappointment are difficult parts of grieving and loss but can be healed by God's grace. I am a living testimony to this healing as well.

Keep in mind, adoption was not an option in Abraham and Sarah's time. A child needed to be "fruit" of the man's loins to be an heir. Surrogate mothering, the option Sarah offers and Abraham agrees to, is the closest thing to our modern-day adoption. Sex with a female slave—who then bears the children of the master—was commonplace and was another way for the married wife to retain her stature in the culture.

 ## He Said

The LORD said to Abraham, "Why did Sarah laugh, and say, 'Shall I indeed bear a child, now that I am old?' Is anything too wonderful for the LORD? At the set time I will return to you, in due season, and Sarah shall have a son."
—Genesis 18:13–14

The story of "father Abraham" is actually a narrative about two people—an elderly married couple who had profound faith in God. Each time I read the Genesis narrative about Abraham and Sarah (who were originally Abram and Sarai) I discover new insights about the nature of faith, as well as questions about marriage, parenting, and laughter. As a man, I am in awe of Abraham's complete trust in God. God told Abraham to move to a new country, and Abraham moved. God told the childless Abraham that he would have a son, and Abraham believed. When God asks Abraham to offer up his son on the altar, Abraham moves in obedience.

I am also aware that at every juncture of this narrative, Sarah enters the picture—the mother of faith, the one who made it all possible. Sarah is mentioned throughout the narrative—sometimes as an equal partner with Abraham, sometimes not—but always she is essential to the outcome. I wonder: Since Sarah would actually give birth to the child of promise, why isn't she lifted up as the exemplar of faith? This seems odd to me.

Men are often at a loss to adequately explain or accept the great power and potential of women. Only a woman can carry a child in her womb. Only a woman can birth new life. Only a woman can carry the promise to its fruition in birth. It has always been so.

In our time, the faith Abraham and Sarah exhibited (Gen. 12—24) has many and far-reaching implications.

For example, many married couples in the United States have difficulty conceiving a first child. We have reasons for this. First, people in general are marrying later in life. Many women feel their "biological clock" ticking as they build a career and stability into their lives. Some couples don't bring children into their family's planning until later, when the "receptivity" to conception is past its peak—for both the man and the woman.

Still the story of Abraham and Sarah continues to hold out the great hope for humanity: that every child is a child of promise and that these promises are not easily conceived, carried, or birthed. The older we are, the more miraculous a birth seems. Likewise, great responsibility comes with the child of promise, as both Abraham and Sarah discover. When have parents not discovered this truth for themselves? The birth is actually much easier than the parenting!

As a man, I am in awe of Sarah. I am also in awe of Abraham. In both Sarah and Abraham I see a great faith, a great trust, and an astounding hope that has stretched down through the centuries and touched me, too.

 # She Said

Sarah laughed within herself, "An old woman like me? Get pregnant? With this old man of a husband?"
—Genesis 18:12 (The Message)

Sarah laughed at God and lived. That gives me hope because I have often (in my most human sin-filled moments) laughed at God's plans for me and wondered if there would be divine retribution some day. Laughing at God and living to tell about it is, indeed, humorous.

Sarah takes the joke further and names her waited-for son "laughter"! Isaac means *laughter*. This woman has guts! It is as if she laughs at God a second time, or perhaps she is laughing at herself.

Since we are made in the image of God, does this mean God has a funny bone too?

I think so. Holy laughter is something I've witnessed many times: during children's sermons in worship or in gatherings where men and women laugh hard and fully in spite of the difficulties and tragedies they are facing. God is laughter's spark, and often our difficulties or perspectives can change after a good chuckle.

Perhaps we take things too seriously. Maybe we need to laugh more. Here our Matriarch and Patriarch model not only obedience to the call but also laughter in the call itself. This laughter exemplifies, perhaps, a resistance to God's work, or doubt, and reveals humor in the impossible predicament of having a child in old age.

Like children, Abraham and Sarah seem to know how to laugh. I hope we can, too.

I love labyrinths. Not long ago I introduced the labyrinth to a group of kindergarten students. Usually, walking a labyrinth is a very quiet, reflective, inner experience. It is, after all, a prayer tool. This experience with the kindergarten students was far from contemplative.

At first the kids thought that the large canvas labyrinth on the fellowship hall floor was a maze. "Not so," I told them. "Mazes get you lost. A labyrinth will never get you lost because it has only one path into the center and the same path back out."

Now these children were intrigued.

A few of them, my daughter included, pretended to be cars and made car noises while moving along the labyrinth path. Some kindergarten students giggled and tickled each other as they moved along the journey to the rose at the center of the labyrinth. Others skipped, hopped, jumped, and ran along the path. They zoomed to the center and then back out again!

When I asked them what they liked the best about the labyrinth, the sentiment was unanimous—the turns! *Ha!*—I thought. If this had been a group of grownups they would have hated the turns and would have wanted a straighter path! (I know this because I have shared the labyrinth experience with adults, too.)

We take ourselves, our callings, and our lives too seriously. When we grow up, we often stop having fun. I wonder: Whatever happened to entering God's kingdom like children at play on a labyrinth's path—just another journey like Abraham and Sarah took?

 # He Said

One central element of the Abraham and Sarah story is the role that laughter plays in the enterprise. The story revels in—among the serious aspects of the situation—a not-easily accepted levity. Large portions of this story are more akin to a joke than a drama.

Abraham was seventy-five years old when God first told him, "I will make of you a great nation" (Gen. 12:2)—a promise that must have sounded ludicrous at the time. The same promise arrived twenty-four years later, when Abraham was ninety-nine (Gen. 17:1). God comes to Abraham by the Oaks of Mamre and reveals that his wife, Sarah, will have a son. Sarah laughs at the idea (Gen. 18:11–15).

The element of laughter is seriously evident throughout. When the child of promise is born, he is named Isaac, which means *laughter* in Hebrew. So there we have it.

But what are we to make of it?

I think this narrative teaches us that faith is most alive, most effective, when it is evidenced by laughter and joy. I'm sure we've all seen our fair share of deadly serious believers—and they generally are not fun people. A dry, sour countenance rarely is a good testimony to God's grace. People who frown as they worship and serve the Lord hardly exhibit the kind of joy we should expect from people who profess to know the living God.

I'm grateful for the laughter of Sarah, especially. Who can believe half the things God has promised us? Our faith, indeed, is wild, untamed, and at times, borderline ludicrous. A God who created both the whale and the dandelion? A God who promises to bless through the tough times? A God who holds out the sanctuary of a heavenly home, a new body, and a new world to come? Surely we can smile at such things—even laugh about them. Incredible!

Years ago, when I was a divinity school student, we used to swap jokes in the lunch room. This break time was always a source of support and camaraderie. Through the laughter we always found truth. I've never forgotten this one:

QUESTION: Do you know the definition of a Puritan?

ANSWER: A Puritan is a person who is bothered by the very thought that someone, somewhere, might be having a good time.

Amen! Sarah knew that.

I wonder what would happen if we didn't take ourselves so seriously? I wonder if, instead of worrying and struggling and positioning, the church might be different if we came together to laugh? Personally, I find laughter a wholesome and life-giving response to God. A great many situations and circumstances in our lives could be improved simply by laughing about them.

Yes, the world is a mess, with much suffering and hardship—all serious stuff. Abraham and Sarah's world fared no better. Still, Abraham and Sarah were people of laughter. They are our examples—our father and mother of faith. How might we use their laughter to transform our families, congregations, and communities through the power of joy?

 # She Said

God also said to Abraham, "As for Sarai your wife, you are no longer to call her Sarai; her name will be Sarah."

—Genesis 17:15 (NIV)

What is in a name? Throughout the Bible several characters, through their calling by God and their commitment to God's causes, experience a change in their names. Today Hollywood actors and actresses change their names because their professional union desires a marketable and unique face. A Hollywood name creates a brand.

In the world of the Bible, names are changed only after God messes in a person's life. The biblical world knows nothing about attention or achieving celebrity status!

Consider Saul and his persecution of the early church. His name change after the Damascus Road experience reoriented his life forever. Saul became Paul, who became a leader and defender of Christ's church. Paul's new name emphasized the new mission and purpose in his life—a life that God in Christ called him to follow!

Jacob was the younger trickster twin who duped his brother and everyone he met. Late one night Jacob, facing another encounter with his brother, Esau, wrestled with God. Injured in the process, Jacob received a new name: Israel. In a deeper reality this new name brought into being a whole tribe, a nation of people. A new people inherited the name that God gives—calling them to fulfill their mission.

This nation of people—Israel—originated from one woman, Sarah. What an honor for this matriarch that our Bible records her name! Recording and remembering the names of women personalities in the Bible is hit or miss. Many women are referred to by their relationship to a father, brother, or husband. Thanks be to God, Sarah is remembered as Sarah. She has her own name, her own place of importance, and her own identity.

A nation cannot be produced unless a woman's womb is involved in the production. Abraham's sperm is not enough to grow a star-filled sky of descendants. How amazing that, for centuries, the part Sarah played in God's plan was so important and significant that the Bible writers never forgot her name.

What amazes me even more is what happened to Sarai's name. Sarai became Sarah through God's intervention. Sarah is one of the few women to have a name change. How cool is that!? God's call came not just to the father of a nation and not just to the mother of a nation but to a married couple. God's call, and Abraham's and Sarah's obedience to that call, influenced this couple forever.

God changes two names. Never before and never since has a couple been affected in such a dramatic way. In this cooperative calling, name changing, and childbearing we can find God's promise and plan for all couples. Here is the gem for you and me and our life partners. We are another link in the chain that connects Sarah and Abraham with their star-filled sky of descendants.

Think about it: Your name relates who you are and what you are about. Your name is more than your identity. Your name can also proclaim your mission statement, your life purpose. For couples, your partnership is a promise of God's blessing, which you share together.

 ## He Said

Here's a novel idea: People who have faith must be willing to move! Well, it's not a novel idea, really. It's an old idea—as old as Abraham and Sarah, as old as the Israelites traveling out of Egypt, and as old as Paul sailing by ship across the Mediterranean to share the gospel of Jesus with the Gentiles. People who have faith are called to a life of movement, not a life of pew-sitting and waiting for the Lord's return.

As a man, I find certain elements of the Abraham and Sarah story to be most unsettling—the idea of being itinerant and transient stands foremost among them. Why can't God just allow me to remain where I am, and as I am? Why this call to journey, to change, to grow from new experiences?

Deep down lies something elemental and important in this call to move. Abraham was called to leave his native land (Gen. 12:1) and to take up residence in a promised land. But this was just the first of many moves. Abraham and Sarah were always on the go. They found no opportunity for standing still, for leading a standard sedentary lifestyle.

What are we to make of this?

Consider your own journey. Where has God taken you? Where have you come from? How far have you come? Are you willing to undertake another journey with God, to tackle a big project, to climb a new mountain, to journey by faith into some uncharted wilderness of the heart or mind? That's what movement is about. That's faith in its essence. Faith is a verb—active, engaged. Our faith is a movement, not an organization.

Looking more deeply into the Abraham and Sarah narrative, I see that God was asking this couple to accept more than a physical journey from one land to another. In some ways, this was the *easiest* transition they made. God was asking Abraham and Sarah to take a journey that would transform their marriage and would shape their love, their parenting, and their future together. God was asking them to take a journey that would transform the world.

God does not ask less of us!

Abraham and Sarah are such great examples because they were willing to go, to move, to be involved. They were not content to stay where they were, or as they were. They wanted what God was offering— but they realized that receiving the full blessing required faith. They had to commit. They were not the kind of people who offered excuses. They accepted and then moved on.

What about us?

When God asks us to go on a journey, to make a commitment, do we offer up excuses? I'm too busy (engaged in other pursuits). I'm too broke (don't have anything). I'm too tired (complacent). I'm too content (I like where I am). We have all offered these common responses to ourselves or to God. Or have we grown into patterns of faith and behavior that offer us no new insights or directions, so that, when God does ask us to step out in faith, we can't even recognize the call?

These are large issues—and all are represented in the Abraham and Sarah narrative.

Father Abraham? Mother Sarah? Thank God they were willing to go. They were willing to trust. They were willing to serve. They were willing to give.

May we be willing to follow in their footsteps!

Discussion and Reflection

1. Share how your child(ren) or lack of child(ren) has contributed positively or negatively to your sense of worth as a person.

2. While God may not have asked you to change your name, how has either the reception of your spouse's name or a nickname been formative or not formative to your sense of identity as a child of God?

3. Share a story that inspired you to learn to laugh at yourself.

4. Where have you experienced God's call to change (employment, location, a decision), and how has it affected your relationship with God?

5. Talk about how faith or the lack of faith affects the promise of being a parent.

6. Take a sheet of blank paper and draw a "map" of your faith journey—including high or low experiences, decisive moments, and the like. Share with your group where and how God has moved along with you.

Chapter 2

Isaac and Rebekah

Genesis 24—28

The family story of our faith continues through Isaac and Rebekah—the next generation. The long-awaited child given to Abraham and Sarah—Isaac—now lives his life in relationship to the promise God had made to his parents. But larger questions emerge. Would Isaac and Rebekah remain faithful to the covenant? What challenges would they face?

Even a cursory reading of Genesis reveals that more is written about Abraham and his grandson Jacob than about Isaac. Isaac's history and exploits are recorded in a mere three chapters—and Isaac in many ways is presented as the connection between Abraham and Jacob (the third generation). The most significant story, perhaps, is found in Genesis 22, where Abraham intends to sacrifice Isaac.

The world of Isaac and Rebekah does tell us about the ancient world of arranged marriages, infertility, parenting practices, and the continuing work of God in human history. We see ourselves in the stories of Isaac and Rebekah. Their foibles and gifts are reminiscent of our own. Their questions are similar to those we ask. Through them, we can even see how God's work continues in us.

 # He Said

When the boys grew up, Esau was a skillful hunter, a man of the field,
while Jacob was a quiet man, living in tents.
Isaac loved Esau, because he was fond of game; but Rebekah loved Jacob.

—Genesis 25:27–28

Sibling rivalry has been a part of the human condition since the beginning. In Genesis 4 Cain killed Abel. From that time, brother has killed brother, and sister has destroyed sister. It's an old story. Much older, even, than the animosity that existed between the brothers Esau and Jacob.

But why? Where and how is this hatred and rivalry born?

Perhaps the story of Isaac and Rebekah can enlighten us further. Here we are introduced to two highly flawed parents. Each parent has his/her favorite son. Isaac, we are told, preferred the wild, elder, hunter son, Esau. Mother Rebekah preferred the domestic, Emeril Lagasse-type Jacob.

Is it any wonder that we see such rivalry and animosity between the brothers? The story of Isaac and Rebekah is a poster example of bad parenting. The scriptures, after all, are not filled with exemplary people held up or heralded as saviors and messiahs. Throughout the Bible we encounter people just like us, people who are flawed, broken, and weak. Isaac and Rebekah fit this mold quite well.

Genesis 26—29 deals with a dysfunctional family, plagued by animosity, deception, lying, cheating, and game playing. Isaac is a strong father, a good provider—but he lacks clarity and has a marginal devotion to those he is supposed to love. Isaac has lost his *laughter,* even though this is his name. Rebekah is a good mother—but she is self-absorbed, angry, and bitter. She complains constantly and looks for every opportunity to take advantage of her husband and eldest son. Esau is a strong man, the eldest, but lacks leadership and moral resolve. Jacob, as his Hebrew name implies ("The Grabber"), is materialistic, deceptive, and easily swayed. Taken together, these family dynamics can only lead to heartache, hatred, and a broken family—and all of it comes to pass as we might expect.

This ancient saga has much to teach us. After all, we live in a highly competitive world. We have been trained and "brainwashed" to believe that only the strong survive, that we must outwit, outlast, and outlive the next guy lest we perish. Even our entertainments reflect our insatiable thirst for competition and winning at all costs. The saga of Isaac and Rebekah, of Esau and Jacob, is as pertinent for us today as it was centuries ago. Their story is our human condition.

We men, perhaps, know more about these truths that we care to express. For many of us, our lives have been dominated by competition on the sports fields from the time we were children. We have carried this competitive thirst into our businesses and cultural mores. We want to be blessed—and we think we have to steal the blessing from someone else to obtain it.

Of course, competition can also press us toward healthier models, too. Faith teaches us that when we strive for the "higher call," when we run the race that has been set before us (Heb. 12:1), or when we engage in warfare against our own demons, we draw closer to God and become better people. By lifting up the broken, strengthening the weak, and caring for the least of these, we demonstrate courage by standing in the gap for others.

The difference, of course, is focus. Isaac and Rebekah reveal one model. But there is another way.

 ## She Said

All of the Genesis patriarchs and matriarchs have bizarre marriages that involve everything from divine visitors, to infertility, to sisterly competition. Isaac and Rebekah's love story has the makings of a great daytime soap opera because it has love, deception, and the challenges of raising very competitive twin boys. Now that sounds like a juicy afternoon television drama!

The courtship—or lack thereof—whets our appetite for all the emotional drama to come. This will be an arranged marriage between two distant family groups, so a servant is sent to fetch a bride for Isaac. The servant, who impresses me as the inspiration behind the matchmaker character in *Fiddler on the Roof*, asks God for a sign to let him choose the proper bride for his master's son. Once chosen, Rebekah doesn't even take the normal ten days to mourn the loss of her family. Instead, she hops on the next camel train and embraces her future.

This Bible story passes over the normal betrothal period of feasting and preparation. All of the wedding and marriage proceedings are so rushed and hurried that no time remains for premartial counseling, bachelor parties, or wedding showers! The reason for the hurried nature of the wedding remains unknown. Bible readers are only told that Abraham is getting old. Perhaps he is hoping to bounce at least one grandkid on his knee.

As Rebekah draws close to Isaac's home, the groom tries to admire her from a distance, but she adds mystery to their meeting by veiling her face from him. Was that a custom or playing hard to get? We can only guess. The Genesis author does reveal to us that Isaac has grieved his mother's death deeply and now finds comfort in his beautiful new bride (Gen. 24:67). This makes me wonder what sort of love and passion Rebekah and Isaac created out of these strange circumstances.

In the dark of his mother's tent Isaac and Rebekah learn about each other and seal the marriage covenant. Scripture says that he loved her (Gen. 24:67). Did Isaac whisper a strange story about his birth? Did he share his father's understanding of being the father of a nation? Did Rebekah laugh at this thought just as Sarah had? We never learn any answers to these fascinating questions; instead, we discover that this couple also struggles with infertility (Gen. 25:21). Rebekah's womb was barren.

Whether it was out of compassion (because he loved his wife deeply) or out of desperation not to disappoint his father, Isaac eventually stands up to God and asks for help (Gen. 25:21). Because God answers his prayer, maybe Isaac's intention is irrelevant. God answers this prayer to the power of two. Fraternal male twins will be the next generation of the covenant promise. The birth of twins would have made a great season-ending cliffhanger for our would-be television soap opera, don't you think?

Even during her pregnancy Rebekah experiences the foreshadowing of what is to come because the children wrestle within her womb. From their birth the boys are radically different from one another. Each son's uniqueness appeals to one parent over the other, which divides this couple so that the marriage bond weakens (Gen. 25:28).

 # He Said

He [Isaac] did not recognize him, because his hands were hairy
like his brother Esau's hands; so he blessed him.

—Genesis 27:23

When I was nineteen years old, my father blessed me in a most profound way. On my birthday, he dropped by the university campus, took me out to dinner, and then invited me to a bookstore to select any title I desired. Doesn't sound so profound, does it? But to a nineteen-year-old college sophomore, it was a day that stands resolute in my memory. This small fatherly act and his gift of time and attention struck me deeply. Our conversation was meaningful. He told me he was proud of me. He affirmed my education and my choice of career. He acknowledged my love of books, of literature, of learning.

In Genesis 27—28 we read about the blessing and the birthright that Isaac gave to Jacob—unknowingly, as it turns out—but a blessing nonetheless. We moderns cannot fully appreciate the gravity of the blessing, which consisted of both a physical touch of the genitals—or literally an oath taken upon the loins and one's future progeny—and also a verbal offer of prosperity. Today, when people read this story, they often wonder: Why didn't Isaac just take the blessing back, if he wanted to give it to Esau instead of Jacob? But in ancient cultures, a man's word was his bond. An oath taken before God was a binding contract. It could not be rescinded. It was a covenant.

Isaac's blessing of Jacob actually set the stage for the whole of Jacob's life. Jacob, the one who had taken his brother's blessing by deceit and trickery, would indeed be blessed in spite of his weaknesses. Later he would take a new name—Israel—and would learn to walk humbly with God and to be a blessing to others (fulfilling the call of Abraham his grandfather).

What might the blessing mean for us today—especially for fathers who desire to bless their children? Is such a thing possible?

Absolutely!

As fathers, we have the capacity to be blessing our children at all times. Our blessing is more than words. Our blessing is the gift of our time, our attention, and also our affirming touch or embrace. Mothers have an equal capacity to bless. We cannot forget that Rebekah shared in the blessing with Isaac; Hannah was the blessing to Samuel; Mary was the blessing to Jesus. So the blessing is not the dominion of the male, but of the parent.

How many single mothers or single dads are the sources of blessing to their children? They are legion. Many more fathers need to step up and offer the blessing of a future and hope to their children.

As we consider our society, we can see that our children need to be blessed by their parents. In spite of their many weaknesses, at least Isaac and Rebekah offered this vision of prosperity and a hopeful future to Jacob. The blessing was not lost. It was not wasted but cherished.

 ## She Said

When the men of the place asked him [Isaac] about his wife, he said, "She is my sister"; for he was afraid to say, "My wife," thinking, "or else the men of the place might kill me for the sake of Rebekah, because she is attractive in appearance."
—Genesis 26:7

Liar, liar, pants on fire! This familiar childhood chant, I hope, was heard on the playground in Isaac's day because clearly within this text, he tells lies. Isaac commands Rebekah to pretend she is his sister instead of his bride. He fibs, not to protect the woman he loves, but to protect himself. Her beauty is so great and tempting that he fears other men will want her. Somehow Isaac perceives he will be safer, have less risk, and retain more power if he lives a charade.

Isaac's actions and attitude reveal quite a bit about his love and protection for his wife. His views of their marriage bond and of her as a person of sacred worth begin to dwindle dramatically after this episode. Somehow, Isaac thinks it would be better for Rebekah to be physically or emotionally abused by strange men in Gerar than for him to suffer the threat of death. As you can see, I get a little peeved about Isaac's decision. What was this guy thinking? In my opinion, Isaac fails to be Rebekah's hero.

God becomes Rebekah's hero and rescues this damsel in distress from her husband's lies. King Abimelech, the ruler of the Philistines, reveals the truth after he catches Isaac and Rebekah in the act of lovemaking. How ironic is that? The king confronts this couple, the charade ends, and no other man touches Rebekah. The lineage from Sarah and Abraham remains pure because of God's divine intervention. Earlier in Genesis, we discover that this is not the first time a male member of this family tells a lie about his wife to protect himself. Abraham did it not once, but twice (Gen. 12:10–12; 20:1–18). So, Isaac learned this sham from the master, his dad. Details around the stories differ a bit, but in both of the former tales Abraham introduces Sarah as his sister to protect himself. In Genesis 20 the author tells us that Sarah is indeed Abraham's half sister. Intermarriage between half siblings was a common practice in those times to preserve the family and tribal community. In Isaac's case, we know the more details about the relationship because of the detailed background regarding Rebekah's and Isaac's courtship. The masculine assumption in all three stories is that a brother could gain more from having an unattached sister than a husband could gain from having a wife. The wife was perceived as a "used" commodity in this male marketplace of power and prestige. Hopefully, our contemporary sensitivities offer us different responses.

We rarely hear this story retold from the pulpit, and yet this encounter tells us so much about ancient gender roles and expectations. Moreover, I think it reveals something deeper about this rocky marriage. We gain another layer of insight that can help us understand why Rebekah manipulated and tricked her aging, blind husband into giving the birthright to the youngest child and not the oldest. While Rebekah didn't necessarily plot her course of action, her trickery may have been a kind of payback for her husband's earlier act of deception. Perhaps there is a hidden lesson here about reaping what we sow.

Clearly, Rebekah has no personal power or privilege. Only through her trickery and manipulative acts does she achieve anything. She uses what she has—the traditional realm of home, hearth, and children—to aid her favorite son in obtaining a blessing and a birthright that was not his to receive. Food and crafty sewing fooled Isaac. We find it most curious that this mom wants for her favorite child—the one who most resembles her—is also part of the Divine will.

 # He Said

When her time to give birth was at hand, there were twins in her
womb. The first came out red, all his body like a hairy mantle;
so they named him Esau. Afterward his brother came out, with
his hand gripping Esau's heel; so he was named Jacob.
—Genesis 25:24–26a

Most of us are sensitive to names . . . or at least name calling. Schools now have "antibullying" codes of conduct for their students, and the era of political correctness has surely saturated most facets of our society. Still, names have power to hurt or to heal, to break apart or to create new. Whenever I read the narratives of Genesis, I am reminded that names have power to define us, too.

Consider, for example, that Rebekah, in Hebrew, means "snare" or "trap" or "cow." Names may not mean so much to us now, but centuries ago, a name defined a person. I wonder how Rebekah lived up to her name, becoming a kind of snare or trap or sleek cow to those she loved. Certainly she trapped Isaac, her husband, and laid in wait until the opportune time to trick him into giving Jacob the birthright and the blessing.

What of Isaac? Yes, his name means laughter, but at least in his latter years Isaac didn't live up to his name. He had become a stale, dried-up man with very little joy in his life. In fact, he was more of a joke than a source of laughter.

When I read about Isaac and Rebekah, I can't help but wonder about the ways we choose to identify ourselves. What is the good name, or the good reputation, that we are living out each day? When people think of you or me, what name—good or bad—might leap to mind? Have we garnered a nickname we have to live down? Or a name of respect we must live up to?

Day by day, year by year, each of us is building a reputation and a memorial—a kind of testimony—to our existence. What will others remember about us? Will our reputation be affiliated with any great causes, any great loves, or any great passions—or will we just be a name on a headstone? What is it we hope to contribute to God's kingdom?

These are large questions—lifelong questions.

Often, we regard our legacies in terms of charitable contributions or having our names engraved on a plaque somewhere, but the greatest legacies we leave behind are carried forward in the hearts and minds of those who follow after. Have we been a blessing to our family and friends? Did we serve and give to the best of our abilities? Did we add to the common good or make the world (or our little corner of it) a better place?

In one way or another, I believe we are all making a name for ourselves. Good or bad. Generous or stingy. Joyous or bitter. Of course, Isaac and Rebekah live on—flawed as they were—through the sacred pages. We get to write our own chapters in God's book, too. We do get to determine how others will remember us.

DISCUSSION AND REFLECTION

1. If you have been married, share the story of the courtship of you and your spouse. If you have not been married, talk about what your parents or grandparents modeled for you about courtship and romance.

2. Lies and deception were part of Isaac and Rebekah's marriage. Consider how that affected their ability to trust or mistrust each other. How have lies been destructive to your most trusted relationships? What has brought you healing?

3. What "right" actions or attitudes did your parents give to you? What did they fail to do right? Discuss how you and others can learn from both the blessings and the failings of your parents.

4. Share how a legacy of blessing from one generation to the next is part of your family's tradition.

5. How do you want others in your family to remember you and your name?

6. How might a faith community model "family" better than our traditional concepts of family?

Chapter 3

Jacob and Leah and Rachel

Genesis 29—33

The patriarch and matriarch narratives culminate in the third generation with Jacob and his two wives, Leah and Rachel. Once again, we see the humanity of these three. Trickery, sibling rivalry, and marriage traditions are significant themes in the Jacob, Leah, and Rachel saga. Their twelve children mark the beginning of the twelve tribes of Israel.

Both the rapid numerical growth of the family as well as their migration into Egypt offer new twists and turns, as we wonder how God's promise to Abraham will be fulfilled. The children of this third generation bring the reader of Genesis closer to the primary events of the Old Testament: the exodus and the law.

Before this family leaves the land of promise, they must deal with treachery and deceit, favoritism and folly. Wrestling might be a primary metaphor here—as this not only describes Jacob's struggle with God at Peniel (Gen. 32) but also the relationships within the family. In spite of their posturing and positioning, however, God remains faithful to the family blessing—and gives abundantly, so that they can be a blessing to others. What a witness of God's loyalty.

 # She Said

So Jacob went in to Rachel also, and he loved Rachel more than Leah.

—Genesis 29:30a

Double dates with your sister sound like a fun idea. My mother and my aunt went on several double dates together when they were in high school. Double dates with your sister are one thing, but marrying the same man, well, that sounds like a really bad idea. It became such a bad idea that later Levitical law forbade it (See Lev. 18). Jacob, Leah, Rachel, and their children learned how bad it was the hard way—by living through it.

Most biblical commentators take ample time focusing on the trickster, Jacob—who is then tricked by his uncle Laban. I would like to focus on the female competition for marital position and male attention. Thus far in the Genesis narrative we have seen how the boys fought among themselves. Now enter two wives who are also sisters. These women offer us a complement to the male-dominated aspects of the narrative.

For example, Jacob and Esau wrestled in the womb together, but Jacob's wives engaged in a birthing war. They too wrestle with each other, struggling to see who will birth more male heirs and who will receive more love from both Jacob and, consequently, in their minds, from God.

Certainly, competition between people can provide a healthy outlet to sharpen skills and can help us learn about how to defend and strengthen ourselves. This type of competition can be healthy and balanced. But what happens when competition isn't healthy? It becomes destructive to both individuals and relationships.

This portion of the narrative helps us to see that girls fight differently than do boys. This little book won't provide enough space for a deep exploration of these differences, but ever since I was in grade school I have noticed that boys battle one way and girls battle in another. For example, when women walk into a room, we typically measure, compare, and evaluate every other woman in that room. I often catch myself doing this very thing. We women are highly competitive—although we may try to hide it beneath quaint

Southern charm or a brash East Coast accent. Regardless of the exterior, women can be ruthless to other women.

Women often betray female colleagues if the opportunity presents itself, or if by doing so, the action will gain a woman an advantage within the male world. Why is it that we women think we need to take out our competition (i.e., each other) to be heard, valued, and understood? We seem to perceive a scarcity in the relationship marketplace for male attention and recognition.

In my own personal history, I can see how female competition played a role in my ordination interview within The United Methodist Church. One of the women interviewing me was especially tough. She grilled me over and over again until a male interviewer finally redirected the conversation. Several weeks later, another male interviewer apologized to me for his female colleague's behavior. "I just don't understand what got into her," he told me.

I knew "what got into her." This colleague's behavior was nothing new to me. I knew it was what we girls have been doing to each other in junior high bathrooms and in adult boardrooms for years. Sometimes we will do it in the name of "seeing what she's made of" or "making sure she knows how to defend herself." We still do it.

Moreover, I have always felt that women in the churches I have served are typically more critical and scrutinizing of me as a woman, wife, mother, friend, cook, housekeeper, and pastor than the males in the church. Oddly, I would have thought that I would have experienced more difficulties with men being able to accept me as their first female pastor. Not so. More often than not, women are the toughest audience in the church—as far as approval of other women goes.

I believe this ancient competitive duel between Rachel and Leah is still with us. We need to quit this ridiculous competition and find other ways to support, encourage, and empower one another to be successful.

 **He Said**

Sure I'm a man, but I'm going to take a risk and comment on the women's issues that I see at play between Leah and Rachel. I'll state my observations, and the women can call me to task if I'm out of line.

I note an intense animosity between sisters Leah and Rachel as soon as they married Jacob. Perhaps this guy just brought out the worst in them, but I also see something dark and twisted in their relationship with each other and in the way they each lusted after power and position (Gen. 30:1–12).

As soon as Leah began having children, she used her motherhood as a powerful tool against her younger sister, who was having difficulty getting pregnant. (Yes, I know this can be the man's problem, but bear with me.) Leah began making fun of her sister because she was "barren." Rachel, on the other hand, knew that Jacob loved her more, and she held this up as a point of scorn to the older sister.

Not much sisterly love here, no deeper concern that would make the Jacob clan a happy family. Leah used her own children as her leverage. Rachel used Jacob's love. Neither won. Both lost. At the center of this animosity are pregnancy and a man's attention. Leah wanted children for leverage. Rachel wanted children as proof that Jacob loved her.

I wonder how this story speaks to many women today. It seems to me that so many women, like Rachel, are still trying to find their purpose and meaning in a man. If they don't have a man's attention or his watchful eye, they feel worthless, powerless, and alone.

Many other women (married or not) clasp onto one paramount desire—to get pregnant. (If you don't think this is true, just examine the statistics.) Now, God knows I love my wife and children. I can't (and don't want to) imagine my life without them. But I think something deep and personal resonates through the relationship between Leah and Rachel. In Leah and Rachel, perhaps, women can see their own lives mirrored in a culture that still values the male above the female, where, often, the only leverage a woman has in marriage, divorce, or life is her children. Or perhaps this warped relationship leads us all (male or female) to the realization that we are seeking acceptance, intimacy, and love—and not power at all. Maybe at this point we begin to draw our value and meaning from a relationship with the Creator.

I guess, as a man, I'm not sure why being single or childless is so heavily stigmatized. Or is it? If women were comfortable with being single, wouldn't those online dating and compatibility sites go bankrupt? If men were comfortable with being single, wouldn't they stop working so hard to gain a woman's attention?

This Leah and Rachel relationship—and their Jacob—has a great deal to it. The saga speaks to where we are and what we need to give our lives purpose and meaning. I'm not sure the narrative, ultimately, has anything to do with pregnancy or marriage at all.

Or is this just me?

 ## She Said

Laban was off shearing sheep. Rachel stole her father's household gods.

—Genesis 31:19 (The Message)

The dueling sisters lay aside their feud at a very critical moment in the Jacob story. Leah and Rachel end their birthing competition, rally together, and agree to a common plan. They acknowledge their husband's work history for Laban and his heavenly vision and begin to show loyalty to their husband and not their father. Their words about their father echo the words of God:

> Rachel and Leah said, "Has he treated us any better? Aren't we treated worse than outsiders? All he wanted was the money he got from selling us, and he's spent all that. Any wealth that God has seen fit to return to us from our father is justly ours and our children's. Go ahead. Do what God told you." (Gen. 31:14–16; The Message)

The daughters of Laban are so critical of their treatment by their father that they eventually see that they are exploited, dispossessed property. They see that their father has not treated them justly. This rare moment of sisterly unity occurs within this polygamous marriage to dramatically separate one generation from another.

The breaking apart of this intergenerational familial group further completes the call of God and draws the new family unit back to the promised land. Leaving Laban and his country behind, Jacob's lineage is now free to continue the work of God in the promised land. The saga's return theme also brings a new confrontation between the two feuding brothers, Jacob and Esau.

Before the brothers meet, Rachel has one final trick up her sleeve. Again, treachery runs deep in this family. After all, Rebekah and Jacob had tricked Isaac. Laban had fooled Jacob, and Jacob later fooled Laban. The last joke goes to the girls. As they are leaving, Rachel fools her own father, Laban. Can you imagine the practical jokes this family played on one another if they did this sort of nasty stuff too?

On their way out of town Rachel steals her dad's *teraphim*. Scholars cannot decide whether teraphim were household gods or ancestor worship statues. What we can confirm is that they were Laban's property. He was more upset about them being stolen than anything else (Gen. 31:30). Laban chases after the family and confronts Jacob—who declares that whoever has the idols will die (Gen. 31:32). Laban searches all the tents, including Rachel's. Eventually Laban encounters his daughter Rachel, who is straddling a camel's saddle with the stolen teraphim tucked inside. Rachel refuses to dismount, claiming that it is her time of the month. The reader has to chuckle at the humor here. Laban eventually gives up the search.

The irony here is that Rachel's menstrual cycle stops her father in his tracks. The final trick belongs to Rachel, who dupes her father. Her uniqueness as a female eventually dominates the final goodbyes and wins the day over paternalistic power and privilege.

But readers are left with a few questions. Was Rachel's motive to exploit her father, as he had exploited her? Was this a form of retribution? Or was this the method the sisters used to break tradition with their father's gods and religious practices so that they could affirm their commitment to Jacob's faith? Perhaps Rachel's ploy was more about her faith than her monthly cycle.

Regardless, this epilogue provides a clever way to conclude the troubled relationships between Rachel, Leah, Jacob, and Laban.

 **He Said**

In Hebrew, the name Jacob means "The Grabber" or "Cheater, Supplanter." He was all of that. Jacob grabbed Esau's birthright the first chance he had. He grabbed Esau's blessing, too. He also grabbed a great deal of this father's goods. Later, he absconded with most of his father-in-law's flock (Gen. 31:1).

Now here is a man for our time!

We know all about greed, don't we? In our culture we value and judge others in terms of the size of home they live in, the type of car they drive, and the amount of wealth they have. We don't like the poor. We hold the rich and famous up as icons. Everyone wants to be *that*!

Whether it's Wall Street or Main Street, we've all fallen prey to keeping up with the Joneses, to grabbing all that we can, or all that we felt we had coming to us. In the past decade, how many billion-dollar scams have we read about that were generated by greed and the gullibility of people who thought they could get something for nothing. Or how about the proliferation of gambling in America? (It only takes one ticket or a pull on the slot machine to be a millionaire . . . or so we are told!) Grabbing all we can get is part of the American dream. Or so it seems. We want everything we can get for our hard-earned money, too. That's why we "Super-size it!"

Yes, I'm familiar with Jacob. You are, too. He's inside us all. As we read through the Jacob saga, something else begins to unfold in Jacob's life that can be a teaching moment for us. Jacob learned his lessons the hard way, as we often do when we reach the end of the rope and discover that things don't satisfy and that all this grabbing isn't what it's cracked up to be.

Jacob's self-discovery, and his God-discovery, occurred when he was returning "home" to meet his brother, Esau. Jacob was nervous, filled with anxiety. One evening alone by the Jabbok River (Gen. 32:22–32) in a dreamlike state, Jacob encountered a mysterious stranger. They wrestled, and Jacob won. Once again Jacob asks for a blessing. The angelic stranger refuses to give Jacob anything of substance. He gives Jacob a new name. "From now on, you won't be a grabber anymore," the angel says, "you will be called Israel."

Now, here's a switch—a complete about-face. Jacob, the money-grubbing young man, is transformed into the "one who struggles with God"—which is what the name "Israel" means in Hebrew.

How does Jacob respond? When he meets his brother Esau, he embraces him instead of hating him. He gives him great possessions and no longer hoards his worldly goods. He discovers himself by giving rather than taking.

In our time the story of Jacob has great implications, especially for men who derive their value or self-worth from the things they obtain or the toys they buy. When we wrestle with God, we discover that God has another name for us—a better purpose and vision. Instead of one life, we are free to live another.

Ultimately, the story of Jacob is about a life transformed. Jacob is no longer self-serving; he is a servant. He is no longer grabbing, but blessing. He is no longer a solitary life wandering the desert with his own clan, but the leader of a community. He is no longer a cheater, but one who gives and loves.

When we truly encounter God, the same transformation can happen to us.

DISCUSSION AND REFLECTION

1. Did you agree or disagree with the idea that boys fight differently than girls? Why or why not?

2. What do you think was Rachel's motive in stealing from her father?

3. How can couples better balance their work with their marriage relationship?

4. In what ways do our human relationships influence our relationship with God?

5. Share a story about someone who was transformed from a "grabber" into a servant.

6. Share a story about an event or decision or moment that defined what kind of family yours would be.

Chapter 4

Joseph and Potiphar's Wife

Genesis 39—50

The book of Genesis culminates in the story of Joseph's bondage in Egypt, his release and ascension to power, and his deliverance of the land and people. The final eleven chapters of Genesis are some of the most powerful we find anywhere in scripture. The contemporary mind encounters great difficulty seeking to understand the powers at play in this ancient culture. Slavery, power over life and death, and the god-like status afforded to the Pharaohs are difficult to comprehend in any modern equivalents.

The Joseph saga ends with reconciliation and the covenant of God intact. Joseph saves the world and his own family. We wonder: What will happen after Joseph dies and the powers of Egypt forgets the blessing of Joseph?

 He Said

Now Joseph was handsome and good-looking. And after a time his master's wife cast her eyes on Joseph and said, "Lie with me."
—Genesis 39:6b–7

Pastors often hear a common confession from men: *I've had an affair.* Usually, the man tries to justify the cheating.

"My marriage wasn't working, and the other woman gave me the attention and affirmation I needed."

"I didn't mean for it to happen . . . it was just one of those things."

"We worked together at the office, and one thing led to another."

"She was nearby."

Indeed, proximity can often be at the heart of many affairs. Men and women don't typically meet through long-distance conversations or sightings—though with the advent of the Internet and online dating services, people can have extended and intimate conversations long before meeting face-to-face. But temptations are usually close at hand—not far away.

From a male perspective, it's easy to see how Joseph was placed in an extremely awkward position. Here he was—a powerful man of Egypt, who had essentially been handed the keys to his employer's house. Potiphar trusted Joseph and gave him carte blanche access to his personal affairs, including daily interaction with his wife. It's easy to imagine how uneasy Joseph might have felt as he made his daily, appointed rounds. He wasn't at the office. He worked in another man's house. He wasn't commuting to work. He labored daily in the palatial spread built by other hands. Most certainly, he had daily contact and conversations with Potiphar's wife. Formal at first. Then casual. And finally a bit more personal.

Joseph was handsome. Or, as the Genesis text explains it in double entendre—he was both "handsome" and "good-looking." A double-whammy. One might even conclude that Joseph was something of a ladies' man—or could have carried himself that way. At any rate, Potiphar's wife was drawn to Joseph. We assume because of his looks—but perhaps because of more.

My wife and I have had many conversations over the years about the forces that draw men to women, and women to men. One of my theories (she always laughs at my theories) is that many women are drawn to men who have power, authority, or wealth—far more than they are to a man's appearance or personality. I may base my assumptions (or are they sexist beliefs?) on news stories, on tabloid fodder related to movie stars and famous CEOs, or on personal observations—but I think we have all seen beautiful women pursing wealthy or powerful men who look like sheepdogs. Something about power attracts the opposite sex. This situation likely holds true for men as well as women.

Regardless, Potiphar's wife certainly found Joseph attractive—and his power and authority was a part of that attraction. Joseph knew it, too. The Genesis narrative actually says, "After a time she cast her eyes on him." It took her awhile to warm up to him, or maybe she was too busy managing her millions—but eventually she took note of the hunk hanging around the house.

From a man's perspective, Joseph may have secretly found Potiphar's wife attractive for these same reasons. She was a powerful woman. Rich. Beautiful—we may assume. Probably quite the catch when Potiphar walked her down the aisle. Their respective positions of power were one of the attractive elements in their proximity and relationship. At first it was just business. Then it became something more—at least to Potiphar's wife.

I have to give Joseph credit, though. He didn't melt under the pressure. Just because she was gorgeous, powerful, and attentive didn't mean he gave in. But I sense he wasn't looking for other employment opportunities, either.

Something about Joseph and this narrative makes a man uncomfortable. Perhaps we see too much of ourselves in this story. Or maybe we are envious of what Joseph had initially—nice living quarters, a great salary, fringe benefits. Though it's ancient Egypt, it's not so far away from any big business opportunity or employment offer. Joseph enjoyed job security—and perks. It's one of those biblical narratives that usually make men angry, particularly those who have found themselves in tempting situations while working the perfect job or earning the large salary. We wonder: Why can't a guy just have a nice job without having to deal with all the sexual opportunities and the tensions?

We blame the wife. The situation. The office environment. It's our custom. Or maybe it's human nature.

 ## She Said

She caught him by the cloak and said, "Come to bed with me!"
But he left his cloak in her hand and ran out of the house."
—Genesis 39:12 (NIV)

Why can't Joseph keep his clothes on? I find it fascinating that at two key moments in the Joseph story his clothes come off. In the first naked act, his older brothers, in a fraternal hazing ritual, strip little Joey of his special coat and throw him in a pit. Here in the unsuccessful seduction by Potiphar's wife, Joseph's nakedness leads to his imprisonment. Someone, please, tell Joseph to keep his clothes on his body! Bad things happen when he is naked!

Considering his family background of polygamy, Joseph's battle with nakedness begins to make sense. Family counselors, psychologists, and education specialists all agree that children learn their sense of sexuality (emotional and physical intimacy) from their families of origin. Our parents modeled and taught us their values about sexuality. You and I do that or will do that with our own children. This was true with Joseph's family.

You don't have to look very hard to realize that healthy contemporary sexual values are completely lacking within the Genesis family narratives. Modern therapists would have a fun time counseling this family!

Polygamy during Joseph's era was very common and deeply complex. Husbands had multiple wives to increase the odds of more children surviving infancy and childhood. The family tree would be strengthened and maintained with all these additional children. Joseph's father Jacob had two wives, Leah and Rachel. Jacob also had children with each of their personal assistants, Zilpah and Bilhah. Thus our Joseph grew up having one father, one mother, three stepmothers, one full sibling, and a dozen half siblings. Talk about complex! Can you imagine the holidays at that house?

Beyond his father's practice of polygamy, Joseph's siblings get into their own sexually complicated predicaments. Let's consider a female member of this family: Dinah, Joseph's half sister. She was raped by Shechem. Here, an interesting question comes to my mind. Why are women only discussed in this family's narrative when it pertains to sex? Nevertheless, Dinah's brothers rescue her. The brothers, on the eve of Dinah's wedding day, trick Shechem (the groom) and his family (and the entire town!) into being circumcised.

While Shechem and his male friends have ancient ice packets on their private parts, Dinah's brothers, Simeon and Levi, slaughter Shechem and his father with a sword. The rest of Joseph's brothers plunder the town and return home with Dinah.

Where was Joseph during this bloody affair? We never learn what part Joseph played, or didn't play. Did he agree with the massacre or refuse to participate because he was opposed to it? We never learn anything more. Yet one thing remains certain. This family is passionate and violent!

One final anecdote about Joseph's family needs to be told because this would shock even the sexually promiscuous guests on *The Jerry Springer Show*. Rachel, Joseph's mom, dies while giving birth to Joseph's only full-blooded sibling, little Benjamin. After her death, Reuben, Joseph's half brother, rapes Rachel's handmaid Bilhah. (Remember, Reuben is the eldest son and is *the* role model for his siblings.) What a strange way to exhibit grief! Reuben chose to assert his role and power in the family by forcing himself sexually upon his stepmother, Bilhah, the mother of Dan and Naphtali. We never learn if Bilhah's sons, who are also Reuben's half brothers, seek their vengeance. Was this another Shechem affair? It is clear however that Joseph remains the hero of his generation. Joseph's honorable choices distinguish him over and above his eldest brother, Reuben.

What a family! Makes me wonder who explained the birds and the bees to young Joseph? Or did anybody? "Who sleeps alone?" is the least asked question in this story.

 ## He Said

In 1993, Michael Crichton (author of *Jurassic Park*) wrote a best-selling book dealing with sexual discrimination in the workplace. *Disclosure*, however, wasn't your typical novel exploring this familiar theme. Rather, *Disclosure* reversed the roles—this time placing a woman in a position of authority—telling the story of a man who found himself being sexually pursued and discriminated against by his aggressive, female boss. The book hit a nerve with readers and was made into a successful movie starring Demi Moore and Michael Douglas.

In *Disclosure*, Crichton manages to weave a narrative of role reversal and sexual temptation that is mildly reminiscent of the Joseph saga. The book explores not only sexual temptation but also many contemporary ideas and mores related to men and power, women and powerlessness and how society has dictated the meaning and significance of these roles. What happens when women have power and men don't? What happens when the woman is the boss and the man has to submit to her authority? What happens when a man doesn't want the sexual advance in the workplace, but the woman does?

Crichton offers these questions up in a lively and provocative way, questions we find increasingly in a work setting where the traditional power roles are reversed or where women are affirmed for their gifts and leadership abilities. As Crichton's novel reveals, men can feel threatened and disrespected (just as women do) when they are placed in subordinate positions and offered promotions based on sexual favors.

In *Disclosure*, the man feels reduced as a male, as if his sex and sexuality are just rungs on a ladder for his female boss to climb. He ends up feeling exploited and used, with nothing to fall back on. Who would believe him if he told others in the company about her aggression? Wouldn't others just laugh? Who would believe that a man could feel powerless in a company dominated by a ruthless woman?

The Joseph saga is not so far from our own workplaces. This story is not far off the beaten path of Wall Street or any major corporation in America. There's more here than meets the eye . . . or the brain.

As most men would point out, Joseph was certainly too trusting—and he overstayed his welcome. In many ways, Joseph was foolish to believe that Potiphar's wife would simply stop her pursuit or, given the final outcome, would admit to her own desires. These are nearly universal truths when it comes to affairs of the heart.

One can tune into a dozen television shows (or more) that reveal the depths of the lies and deceptions that people will perpetrate as truth when caught in an act of passion. Court shows, daytime dramas, talk shows (many that deal almost exclusively with extramarital affairs or secret loves), and movies show people persisting in the idea that someone else made them respond as they did or that they are not to be blamed for their actions. Men don't like being blamed for anything, and we certainly don't like other people pointing out our foolishness and our frailties (especially women).

Maybe Joseph thought he could talk his way out of any situation. Power has a way of blinding us in such ways—men particularly. The Genesis narrative persists in the idea that Joseph continued to act as if all was well in the Potiphar household or that he had everything under control, even though it was actually Potiphar's wife who had the true power and the upper hand. When it all came down to her word against his, Joseph suddenly realized that her husband was naturally going to believe *her*.

This reality brings us to another subtle man's perspective on this story—and a question that has plagued men for centuries. Why do men believe they can outthink women? In my experience, women have far greater intuitive powers than men—and when it comes to relationships, they have much deeper, richer, and forceful insights than men do. Maybe it's because they listen more closely or talk more completely about themselves and their feelings. It's rare that you ever hear men talking deeply about anything—especially on the personal or emotional level. Whatever it is, a husband will almost always trust his wife if it comes down to her word against the word of another man. Joseph didn't see that one coming—and he should have.

 ## She Said

She called out to the members of her household and said to them, "See, my husband has brought among us a Hebrew to insult us! He came in to me to lie with me, and I cried out with a loud voice; and when he heard me raise my voice and cry out, he left his garment beside me, and fled outside."
—Genesis 39:14–15

With these family bedroom activities going on around him, I am curious to know what Joseph learned. What did he retain about respect for women, emotional intimacy, and sexual boundaries within family or about coworkers and future boss's wives? How could he learn if he was busy watching his father and brothers in their sexual exploits?

It must be a God thing that Joseph holds back from responding to Potiphar's wife's advances, because it seems as if every other male in his family would have. Maybe that is the point of this story. Clearly, no one in this family has any idea of appropriate boundaries! Yet, in spite of his highly dysfunctional family, sexually complex role models for relationships, good looks, charm, and intelligence, Joseph knows enough not to get into bed with his boss's wife. Way to go, Joe!

Now, it should be noted that Joseph was still caught with his clothes off. Let us not forget that! Considering the woman's insecure position of influence and affluence, Joseph's battle with nakedness makes even more sense.

While living in North Carolina for three years, I learned that there is a difference between "naked" and "nekkid." "Naked" (pronounced NAY-ked) is when you singularly are wearing your birthday suit. "Nekkid" (pronounced NEK-id) is when you and someone else are wearing only your birthday suits. Therefore it does take two, after all, to get "nekkid." Let's focus on these two, Potiphar's wife and Joseph, for a moment.

What do we know about Potiphar's wife? The most striking thing about the story is the silence. We never learn her name. She is known to us only through her role as a wife and the possessive apostrophe with a letter *s* next to her husband's name. The woman in this story is the only person not given a name. At least her name is never recorded. That is striking. Refusing her a name means refusing her power, personality, and identity. Only players with bit roles go unidentified.

The absence of a name for Potiphar's wife (even though other women's names in the Genesis narratives are recorded) speaks volumes. One would have assumed that a detail like a name in a story about nakedness and legal or criminal accusations in the workplace would be important enough to include. For our biblical writer the individual may not have been a matter of significance, only the role she played.

Her lack of name is only the tip of the iceberg. Her situation is much more uncertain and unstable. A woman in the ancient world had no legal rights, no inheritance privileges, and therefore no means to support herself beyond what she gained from her husband. A female was considered the property of her husband.

The Bible makes sure we know that Potiphar was considered very wealthy. Thus the wife had access to wealth, although it was not her own. Her husband was smart and financially savvy enough to hire excellent staff (i.e., young capable Joseph) so that Potiphar could "have no concern for anything but the food that he ate" (Gen. 39:6). Her wealth, her fine house, her servants, and staff were all extensions of her husband's power, authority, and position as the head of the household. The wife had nothing, not even her own name.

Even more crucial to her position in the household, her status and prestige as a child-bearer, to provide an heir for her husband, remains unknown. No children are mentioned in this story so we wonder how precarious and perhaps even fragile was her status in the Potiphar household. Was her seduction a way to get pregnant? A pregnancy could have meant greater security for her within the household. Or it could have gained her freedom through a divorce. We shall never know.

On the other side of this relationship equation is Joseph, the young foreigner, God-believer, and indentured servant. His ethnicity and race made him stand out in any Egyptian crowd. Joseph had no personal financial means or wealth to back him up. Joseph's brothers had sold him. He was alone, left to use his wits and God's grace to gain opportunity and influence. His only asset in comparison to Potiphar's wife was his gender as a male.

What intrigues me about this story is the unequal distribution of power between Joseph and Potiphar's wife. To our contemporary ears, this is a story about sexual harassment. Sexual harassment, we know, is about power and the dynamics of power in a relationship, not sex. There are even different types of sexual harassers. What of Potiphar's wife? Is she a predatory harasser who gets sexual thrills from humiliating others? Or is she a dominance harasser? Or is she a territorial harasser, who seeks to maintain privilege in jobs or physical locations?

 # He Said

When his master heard the words that his wife spoke to him, saying, "This is the way your servant treated me," he became enraged.
—Genesis 39:19

Not long ago, during a conversation with some friends in a coffee shop, someone pointed out that it is still more socially acceptable for a man to have an affair than it is for a woman to be unfaithful. His point was—women are more stigmatized than men are if they *do* have affairs. In some cultures, he said, it's almost accepted that men will have mistresses. It's okay, as long as they don't get caught. Now, I'm not an expert on cultural mores (nor am I defending having mistresses), but I found his insight intriguing.

Is there something in the Joseph saga (as it relates to the episode with Potiphar's wife) that lends itself to sexism? Do we tend to see Potiphar's wife in a less favorable light because of her lust than, say, King David (and his affair with Bathsheba) or Samson (and his womanizing)? Do we let Joseph off the hook too easily and just say that he was in the wrong place at the wrong time?

Again, men tend to extrapolate a great deal from a story like this. The story seems to expose the baggage of mistrusts that some men may carry about women.

As I was writing this chapter, I happened to be listening to a talk show in which two African American pastors were debating acceptable dress for a woman. One was expounding on the idea that women naturally send a message to men based on how they dress. The other was laughing at this notion.

"If a woman dresses suggestively or reveals too much," the first pastor said, "men get the idea that she will say 'yes' if they offer an advance. They think that, even if she says 'no,' she doesn't really mean what she says. Her dress is sending a different message."

"But men can send the same message," the other pointed out. "What about the baggy pants, the tight shirts, and so forth? Just because a woman dresses sharply or smartly doesn't mean that she's easy."

Debates over dress reign eternal. Proverbs contains many citations regarding the dangers of looking at beautiful women that suggest averting the eyes from those who dress suggestively or wear makeup (Prov. 5). In letters to the early churches Paul and early Christian writers gave instructions on dress and deportment (1 Tim. 2:8–10; Titus 2:3–6). Questions about dress and style occupied people in earliest biblical times.

Was Joseph flaunting his "good looks" too much? Even if he were, does that represent an invitation to sexual advance? These are loaded questions, really, questions the church has never fully addressed. Some traditions, such as the holiness tradition, have attempted to make moderate dress, conservative hairstyles, and little or no jewelry or makeup principal marks of one's humility and piety. When I was a teenager, my friends and I used to try to establish the denomination affiliation of the women in town just by looking at their hairstyles and the dresses they wore. It was teenage sexism at its finest hour—and we were frequently correct in our assessments. But the mores and social patterns have certainly changed. Does dress say anything about our faith? How about the cars we drive? The homes we live in? Perhaps these are only peripheral concerns of the Joseph narrative and the biblical mandate to be a "light to the world," but these questions certainly provide some insight into the allure that a woman could feel for a man, or a man for a woman. Today, with the rise of "prosperity gospel," many make the assumption that people of faith (or who truly *have faith*) will be wealthy, healthy, and successful in every way.

The Joseph narrative raises many questions for men about the nature of power and possessions—even if they are peripheral concerns in the story. Could it be that, while Joseph wasn't attracted to Potiphar's wife, he was certainly captivated and seduced by the things she possessed? The real turn in the saga may not have been the accusation of Potiphar's wife, but the fact that Joseph suddenly found himself on the other side of prosperity. Suddenly he was back in jail—penniless and abandoned.

The larger question—and the one at the heart of this story—is this: Would Joseph remain faithful to God even if he lost everything? From a man's perspective, this is the toughest question. What happens when a man has to pay for someone else's mistake—and a woman's mistake to boot? Will he fold up like a cheap suit, or stand in the fray and trust God? Will he lash out and try to get even, or will he forgive and move on? Will he mistrust women for the rest of his life, or will he see women in all of their beauty, giftedness, and grace and learn to love again?

Many jilted men, or betrayed lovers, or heartsick husbands have to ask these questions of faith and of character. They define who we are and who we will become—as men.

Joseph seemed to emerge on the other side with his faith and trust intact. He learned from his experiences. He became older and wiser. But he didn't stop loving women and treating them with respect.

May we men be found as faithful as Joseph.

 ## She Said

Sexual harassment is as common today as it was years ago. Thousands of sexual harassment cases jam U.S. courts each year. Thousands of cases are brought to the Equal Employment Opportunity Commission (EEOC) annually. More and more numbers of those cases were filed by men against their female supervisors. Women as well as men can abuse their role, power, and influence.

What about Potiphar's wife? Did she abuse or misuse? Did she have a thing for young, good-looking, efficient Jewish boys from up north? Is she the abuser, the victim, or something else entirely? Power in a sexual relationship touches on the issue of consent. Is the sexual contact desired or wanted by the recipient? Reverend Patricia L. Liberty, the executive director of Associates in Education and Prevention in Pastoral Practice (AEPPP), affirms that for sex between two adults to be sex and not a crime or immoral act, both must consent. She writes, "In reality, consent is far more complex. In order for two people to give authentic consent to sexual activity there must be equal power."[1] Clergy, for example, cannot be in an equal position of power with their parishioners because of moral and spiritual authority, education, community respect, public image, and so on.

Joseph was not a rabbi—and therefore not clergy—but the ideas of consent and power in this affair are intriguing. Let's look more closely at the scene in Potiphar's house. Who had the power? Obviously, the answer is Potiphar. Everyone in this story answers to him and his authority. However, in the relationship between Joseph and Potiphar's wife, who has more or less power? Here things get tricky. I think that is precisely why this story ended with Joseph's incarceration. The battle is one of power and not necessarily a sexual battle.

Potiphar's wife has power through the good graces of her husband. Because of her gender as female, she is not Joseph's equal. Nor is she considered an equal to any man. She may have been physically attracted to and/or emotionally enamored by Joseph. However, her lack of personal status as an equal to Joseph makes any sexual encounter between them nonconsensual. Sex between these two would have been anything other than an affair between love birds. Where equality is lacking, sexual harassment, sexual violence, and interpersonal power take over.

---

1. Reverend Patricia L. Liberty, "Why It's Not an Affair," http://www.aeppp.org/affair.htm.

Joseph's power came from his boss. Joseph was not an equal to his boss's wife. He was a foreign indentured servant in their home. Joseph could have had sex with the wife if he wanted to, but their sexual encounter would not have been a mutual fling. Sex by Joseph's initiation would have been considered dominant and aggressive, which explains why her cry of rape sounded realistic and got the husband's attention. The unequal distribution of power and status in this relationship makes sex by either one's invitation anything but a mutual affair.

What happens when two people, who are not in positions of power, have a relationship? They do what all of us do. They have a strategic battle for self-confidence, position, influence, and dominance. One pushes the other, and the other pushes back. Clearly from this account, the wife started the push-pull. She initiated the dance of power.

I have to wonder about Potiphar's wife's true motives. History has not been kind to her, painting her as an oversexed vixen who affirms the tawdry image St. Augustine had of women. St. Augustine would have thought of her as a typical seductress, out to bring down a godly man.

Was she oversexed or underloved? Was she bored or lonely? Or was she simply trying to test the imbalance of power in her house? I wonder if she was manipulative, but not in the manner church history has treated her. My speculation is that the wife played a little game and had a little fun with Joseph, at his expense of course.

A familiar Egyptian folk legend called the "Tale of the Two Brothers" recounts a similar story. An upright man works faithfully for his older brother only to be propositioned by his brother's wife. The young man refuses, the woman cries rape, and the man flees. Sound familiar? It is the story line of our tale. Potiphar's wife may have known this story. Did she play out the script to get rid of Joseph and restore the dynamics in her home? Or did she have a thing for young Jewish boys? Hard to say, but the striking similarity adds another layer of intrigue to our tale.

The sad part of this story is that poor Joseph had to suffer the consequences for something he did not initiate nor participate in. His sexual harasser is never jailed. But Potiphar's wife might argue that her marriage is a prison in itself. No matter, Joseph is the one thrown in jail (how ironic!). He's in another pit again! He is forced to live out the consequences of the power struggle between his boss's wife and himself.

After the story, we never learn anything more about Potiphar, his wife, or their marriage situation. The story rolls on, and God's grace moves again in Joseph's life so that he is in a position where he could have influence and opportunity to save and, ultimately, be reconciled with his dysfunctionally complex family.

Moreover, scripture doesn't tell us much about Joseph's own marriage. We don't learn if he was a good or bad husband. We know that Joseph was later rewarded for his good work with a wife, Asenath, the daughter of a priest. She gave him two sons, but that is all the Bible tells us. Was Joseph faithful? Did he take an additional concubine? No other wife or children are mentioned. Were Joseph and Asenath happy? Did she ever try to cheat on him? Were they close friends as well as lovers? We never really learn.

We do learn the results of Joseph's incarceration. I marvel at God's will for Joseph's exile in prison. It is unjust that he suffered because of a false accusation, yet a special aspect to this part of the story is rarely affirmed. Solitude and silence are "wonder twins" of personal maturity and spiritual growth. All of the Christian saints and mystics agree about the transformative power of silence and reflective solitude. I have heard it said that God's language is the language of silence.

In jail, Joseph experienced more solitude and silence than most people do. He had plenty of time to ponder all of his relationships: his family, his former boss, and his boss's wife. There would have been long periods of time to reflect, process, and perhaps even learn from his past. In any case, I believe that Joseph used his imprisonment wisely, making the most of the life lessons that God had been teaching him.

Again, I say, way to go, Joe!

DISCUSSION AND REFLECTION

1. How is it possible for men and women to work in proximity with each other without tensions? Explain.

2. What do you think the relationship is between power and attraction? Wealth and attraction?

3. How have you experienced women and men in power roles? Does one gender fare better than another? Why or why not?

4. Who receives a harsher stigma if unfaithful to a spouse: men or women? Why?

5. What aspects of the Joseph narrative with Potiphar's wife did you find most enlightening?

6. What aspects of this Bible story do you see present in our society (news, workplace, business, etc.)?

Chapter 5

Moses, Miriam, and Aaron

Exodus, Numbers 19–21

Exodus is, essentially, a book about God's deliverance. Following the death of Joseph, life in Egypt changed dramatically as years passed and new Pharaohs came to power. To rescue the people—who have become great in number—God needs a new plan and new heroes. God needs a whole family of champions to deliver the people from slavery.

Enter Moses, Miriam, and Aaron

Among the most illustrious personalities in history, Moses stands alone among the Hebrew people. Moses' influence and personality are so great, the first five books of the Bible (the Torah) are attributed to him as author. Early chapters of Exodus detail the special circumstances surrounding Moses' birth and show him set apart from a young age to serve God's plan.

Moses does not lead by himself. He is aware of his inability to speak well (Ex. 4:10) and God offers Moses the assistance of his brother, Aaron, to serve as spokesman (Ex. 4:14). Later, as the people flee captivity and exit the land of Egypt, Miriam, Moses' sister, leads the celebratory dance after the deliverance at the Red Sea (Ex. 15:20–21). So she becomes a leader as well.

Now, let's take a closer look at how one family helped God bring a whole people out of slavery and oppression.

47

 # He Said

The exodus drama is the story of a people—chosen, called, and redeemed. It is also a human drama about leaders—and more specifically, about flawed leaders.

We don't generally like our leaders to be flawed. We prefer perfection. Or, at the very least, we prefer leaders who will do it our way, or tell us what we like to hear. Leaders with scars or leaders who have obvious weaknesses are easy to dismiss.

In times past, the flaws of leadership were not as easily noted. Gossip was about the only way to bring out the skeletons in the closet. Today, with the proliferation of media, with background checks, private investigators, and cameras and tape recorders in every room, leaders have few places to hide. Weakness from even the distant past can be exploited. In our day, it is easy to find the weakness in another person and then make that weakness even larger.

The leaders of the exodus—first Moses and then Aaron and Miriam—were noticeably flawed. Moses, while humble and close to God, suffered from low self-esteem and a lack of confidence. Aaron, while a fluent and forceful speaker, was easily swayed by public opinion and often caved in when emotions were running high. Miriam, while one of the greatest female leaders and a prophet, suffered from visions of self-grandeur and was often too outspoken and aggressive.

Peering into the lives of Aaron and Miriam in particular can be like gazing into a mirror. We see our own reflections in them, especially when we attempt to lead or serve others.

During my first pastoral appointment, I was blessed to have an older mentor—a pastor named Jeff Davis—who took me under his wing and gave me advice. One evening, following a particularly troublesome church board meeting, Jeff invited me over to his house and gave me some advice I've never forgotten. "It's tough being a leader," he said simply. "And the bigger the problems you are trying to overcome, the more opposition you are likely to bump against. Don't worry about your flaws. Rest on your strengths and trust that God will see you through."

I've considered Jeff's advice many times in my life and my ministry. It rings true. Focusing on our weaknesses is easy when we are trying to do great things for God. Our flaws are evident. God is the giver of gifts.

He provides our strengths so that it is imperative that we focus on our strengths. That's where success comes from.

Aaron and Miriam appear too often to focus on their weaknesses rather than their strengths. What would have happened had Aaron done more speaking during the tough times? How different would the exodus experience have been had Miriam prophesied more often?

These are important questions, ones we should all consider during the tough times.

 **She Said**

Then Miriam the prophetess, Aaron's sister, took a tambourine in her hand, and all the women followed her, with tambourines and dancing.

—Exodus 15:20 (NIV)

The parents of Moses, Miriam, and Aaron, I would guess, had a lot of pride as well as a huge parenting challenge on their hands with three children who became leaders on God's behalf! All three of these siblings are referred to as prophets and speakers. Their communities held them in high esteem. To keep his promise, rescue the Hebrew people out of slavery in Egypt, and lead those folks to the promised land, God used the entire generation of one family.

Families link and fulfill the work of God throughout the Old and New Testaments, but rarely does God call and use a whole generation of siblings. We might point to Joseph and his brothers. Joseph, after his brothers sold him into slavery, achieved a position later in life to save his entire family, including those brothers who became the leaders and namesakes of the tribes of Israel. The New Testament tells of sibling sets like James and John, the sons of Zebedee, and Peter and his brother Andrew who serve as disciples of Jesus and leaders of the early church movement.

Vocations and professions often run through a family lineage tree. Some folks are apt to follow in their parents' and grandparents' path for science, medicine, law, religion, or politics, and so on. For many centuries in both Western Europe and the United States, the family business (i.e., the assets as well as the skills and tools of that trade) were inherited from one generation to another. On my father's

Roman Catholic side of the family, a male in every generation has answered the call to vocational ministry as a priest. My ordination as both a Protestant and a female made the most unique generational contribution to our family tree. On my mother's side of the equation we have lived in the United States since before the Revolutionary War as Quakers and farmers. My mother's ordination as a United Methodist pastor broke that family chain.

We need not be surprised then that such a strong and vibrant family of siblings would be a part of God's great plan to move a nation from one place to another. Their mother must have been an awesome home school teacher! This family is indeed special, and we can claim that the exodus was actually a family business.

How healthy and functional was this family business? Birth order could be a clue about this group of feisty siblings. It could give us all sorts of insight into their relationships with each other and how that was played out as adults while wandering through the wilderness. The birth order of the two boys in this family is very clear in Exodus 6:20 and 7:7. Aaron is the eldest male son in this family by three years.

Miriam, while not named in the earlier portion of Exodus, we must assume was older than Moses. How else would she have mediated the exchange between Pharaoh's daughter and her own mother, Jochebed? She was clever even as a young girl to think on her feet to save her brother. Some Jewish legends claim that Miriam is the oldest of all three of Jochebed and Amram's children.

This means Moses is apparently the "baby of the family." Yet God calls baby brother to be the great leader. The Bible consistently reports how birth order means nothing to God because God always rearranges things for God's purposes.

 ## He Said

While they were at Hazeroth, Miriam and Aaron spoke against Moses because of the Cushite woman whom he had married . . . and they said, "Has the LORD spoken only through Moses? Has he not spoken through us also?" And the LORD heard it.

—Numbers 12:1–2

In many ways God made the Exodus from Egypt a family affair. Moses took the leadership role in this defining event for the Jewish people. But still his sister, Miriam, and brother, Aaron, loom large in the unfolding drama. Significant questions remain about the whole family and exactly what their relationships were like.

Let's take Miriam. We first encounter her by name in Exodus 15:20—immediately following the deliverance by the Red Sea, when the Egyptians are drowned. Following Moses' song, Miriam leads the women of the camp in a rousing chorus with tambourines: "Sing to the LORD, for he has triumphed gloriously; horse and rider he has thrown into the sea." Here we learn that Miriam was "Aaron's sister." And for the first time she is called a prophet.

Is this Miriam the same sister who years before protected the infant Moses, who was floating in a papyrus basket in the Nile? Exodus 2:4 just states: "His sister stood at a distance, to see what would happen to him".

Aaron, on the other hand, is mentioned for the first time during a conversation Moses has with the Lord. Moses tries to make a case for his own deficiencies. He tells God he is not the man for the job, for his inability to speak well demonstrates his incapacity to lead. God tells Moses: "What of your brother, Aaron, the Levite? I know that he can speak fluently" (Ex. 4:14a). God finally tells Moses that Aaron will be the voice of the operation.

But how exactly were Moses, Aaron, and Miriam "related"? How were they family? The scriptures are simply unclear in these points. As we read further into the Exodus account, and in particular through the long, tedious forty years of the sojourn in the wilderness, Miriam and Aaron have a more active role—though not altogether satisfactory ones.

In the book of Numbers, odd things begin to happen to this family—that is, to Moses, Miriam, and Aaron. The people complain and groan, as food and water remain scarce. Suddenly bickering among the siblings dominates the scene. Seemingly out of nowhere, Miriam and Aaron conspire against Moses, demanding equal consideration as leaders (Num. 12:1–2). Displeased by this coup, God punishes Miriam with leprosy (Num. 12:10–16). For some reason, Aaron escapes unscathed.

Still, Miriam and Aaron do seem related, as they appear to be cut from the same cloth. Aaron had led the people astray earlier in the exodus, when he allowed them to create the golden calf and worship it (Ex. 32). Both Miriam and Aaron have the weaknesses of pride and ambition.

What can we learn from this dynamic duo?

Much, I think. For example, does family leadership work? Or, perhaps more pointedly, can ministry be passed from father to son, from brother to sister . . . and should leadership be confined to one household?

These large questions include implications woven through our most cherished institutions. Americans have a long history and strong penchant for voting by family name and heritage. The political implications for electing members of the same family have been true for both Democrats and Republicans. Many communities across our country have been, or are, controlled by a small clan of people who bear the same last name. Even in the church, we can find hundreds of examples where leadership has passed along via family ties rather than through merit, giftedness, or service. *Ouch!*

The exodus narrative dredges up some serious questions about leadership and merit. If they had not been "related" to Moses, would Miriam or Aaron have ascended to their positions in the community?

Considering these implications is not easy . . . as often we don't know what to make of our own family history and the "big breaks" we have enjoyed in life. Still, they are worth pondering, aren't they?

 She Said

Miriam and Aaron began to talk against Moses because of his Cushite wife, for he had married a Cushite.
—Numbers 12:1 (NIV)

Family fights! Tabloids, talk shows, best-selling novels, television miniseries—all are filled with squabbles, catfights, and wars between families. So too is the Bible. This verse from Numbers reveals a tinderbox of emotions between the terrific trio. Two siblings worked up about their little brother's choice in a life mate. Sound familiar?

I must admit that I have no life experience on the subject of sibling rivalry and familial feuds. My upbringing was lived as a single kid. My imagination and heart longed for an older brother though. For whatever reason, I always carried the notion that an older brother would be protective and kind and that he would watch out for me. That never came to pass, but I was later blessed with my husband's siblings.

As the outsider marrying into my husband's clan, I have compassion and understanding for Moses' Cushite wife, Zipporah. Did she have to earn and win the affections of her husband's sister, as I have? I learned through both my mistakes and better moments that sisters are very protective of their brothers, especially when it comes to ideas about marriage. My sisters-in-law, though, have been very generous in their affections toward me. What could they say when their little brother chose a preacher as a wife?! That makes me laugh. My appreciation for the unique bond between sisters and brothers has grown because my husband is especially close to his oldest sister, who shares his birthday.

Sisterly protectiveness is not all bad. After all, that characteristic gave Miriam the gumption as a young child to help her brother stay connected to the family. A loyalty bond connects Miriam with her brothers, and vice versa. Although, I have to wonder . . . did the boys put up the same amount of fuss regarding Miriam's future groom?

We do need to acknowledge that women are known to be fiercely competitive with other women. I've witnessed female competition in the classroom as well as the boardroom. So why not within the family system? I wonder if Miriam was spearheading this campaign against Zipporah because she was worried about losing her role in leadership and her position of influence. Perhaps Miriam felt she would no longer be the only female whispering into Moses' ear. Perhaps she felt Moses would now be listening to his wife. But that doesn't completely explain Aaron's objection.

Here the family feud reaches a new depth of dysfunction. The new wife is a Cushite. Ethnically, she is a different race. Moreover, her family shares ancestry with the people who have enslaved the Hebrews all these years. Strike one: Moses married a different race. Strike two: Moses married the enemy.

Moreover, Zipporah's father was a priest in Midian. A tradition outside the Bible portrays Zipporah as following in her dad's vocation as a priest herself. What else would explain the strange scene in Exodus 4:24? Strike three: Moses married a religious leader of another religion. A family coup is formed.

 He Said

Numbers 20 reports three important events—all life-altering—for Moses, Aaron, and Miriam. First, in Numbers 20:1 Miriam dies and is buried in Kadesh. Soon after, the people once again complain about a lack of water. Moses and Aaron gather the people together (Num. 20:9–13), incite the people by calling them rebels, and then Moses strikes the rock twice with his staff to bring forth water. God is displeased, but the reasons are not made clear. The outcome: Both Moses and Aaron are barred from entering the promised land because they did not "trust in the Lord." Soon afterwards, Aaron dies.

Talk about life unraveling!

It is not insignificant that Moses' and Aaron's downfall follow closely upon the heels of Miriam's death. They may have given up. And after the waters of Miribah, Aaron dies too.

Considering Miriam and Aaron in this context, I have to wonder if more than Murphy's Law could have been at play. After all, life can often beat us down and place us in situations and times when we are not at our best. I've always wondered if Miriam's death wasn't somehow the beginning of the end for Moses and Aaron. After all, losing a sister is difficult. She may have been the kind of personality that kept the family together.

Thinking of Miriam reminds me that none of us is replaceable. Not really. Sure, after our deaths, someone will occupy our desk at work, someone else will coach the little league team, and another person will mow the yard. But we are not replaceable to the people who love us or who depend on us for love, nurture, or intimacy.

I see Miriam as vital to the success of the promise. When she dies, Moses and Aaron unravel.

Here is a reminder that, without faith in God, we can quickly fall into despair when bad things happen, or we can go through the motions of life without carrying forward the legacy of those we love. Memory is important, but so is the future. To embrace what lies ahead, we cannot forget where we have come from.

DISCUSSION AND REFLECTION

1. How has a family business or the sharing of the same career path been a part of your family's legacy?

2. Every one of us has stories about family feuds. Let's focus on the positive. Share a story about a family feud that was resolved or a story about how reconciliation was achieved in your family.

3. What are the burdens or blessings of leadership when it comes from within the same household?

4. How have you reconciled your leaders (home, work, family, community, church, or government) and their flaws?

5. Share how you or someone you know has moved forward after a death in the family.

6. How do you see God using families today to move people or communities forward?

Chapter 6

Ruth and Boaz

The Book of Ruth

Though brief, the book of Ruth occupies a much larger place in the Bible than we might at first imagine. The book is strategically located between the books of Judges and 1 Samuel—a position in the canon (the scriptures) that serves as a transition between one time (the age of the Judges) and another (the age of the kings and prophets).

The book of Ruth relates the story of two widows—one older, the other younger—related by marriage. After their husbands die, Ruth decides to venture forward with her mother-in-law, Naomi, and return to Naomi's native land of Judah, though she herself is a Moabitess. The story turns romantic, among other themes, when Ruth meets a wealthy landowner named Boaz, who treats this young, foreign woman with kindness and respect. Boaz agrees to marry Ruth in accordance with Levitical law, which specifies that the next of kin should continue the family name. Ruth and Boaz fall in love and are married. Ruth, the Moabitess, becomes the mother of Obed, the father of Jesse. And Jesse becomes the father of David—the great messianic king.

So, this is not just a love story. It is a theological and genealogical work meant to show the connections between the Gentile nations and God's great work of redemption. It is a book meant to demonstrate that God reserves a blessing for those who help the poor, the widow, and the orphan. It is a book the preserves ancient customs and rites and gives us a glimpse of ancient family life, home, and marriage. Most of all, the book provokes questions.

 # She Said

The servant who was in charge of the reapers answered, "She is the Moabite who came back with Naomi from the country of Moab."

—Ruth 2:6

The *VeggieTales* cartoon version of the book of Ruth, titled *The Duke and the Great Pie War*, does not do justice to this complex book. In the children's version, the subtle nuances of the story are lost when all the vegetables toss cream pies at one another. The cartoon version of Ruth does do one thing well. The animation cleverly portrays the animosity, racial divide, and cultural difference between two peoples—the Moabites and the Israelites. If you have not seen this little movie, you could borrow it from a preschooler.

In the biblical book these racial and ethnic differences are played out on a tapestry full of sharp contrasts: famine and harvest, widowed and married, infertility and fertility. The contrasts give us access to this ancient world from the vantage point of an unmarried woman who remains unprotected and impoverished in this strange land. Women, in this world, could speak, but they had no power otherwise.

As the book of Ruth reveals, without husbands or sons, Ruth and Naomi are left to fend for themselves, and they are bereft of security even within a land of plenty.

Life circumstances for these two single women in rural Judah were complicated further by the contrast between interethnic marriage and those who were married within a closed Judaic system. Ruth is an outcast even as she seeks to remain loyal and compassionate toward her Jewish mother-in-law. Ruth's character remains suspect throughout the story. She is, after all, an alien living inside the promised land of Israel. This theme—the significance of being an alien or foreigner in the land of Israel—is woven tightly inside this story.

Today many such immigrants leave their language and culture and relocate from their homeland, embarking on a long journey to a land that appears to promise financial and personal security. What happens today when two women undertake such a journey by themselves?

Throughout the Old Testament, God commanded the Hebrew people to remember that they were once aliens in a foreign land and therefore were to be compassionate to those who may seem strange, or different or new. Exodus states very clearly the reason why: "'Do not mistreat an alien or oppress him, for you were aliens in Egypt'" (22:21 NIV).

While the theme of welcoming the alien lingers within the story of Ruth, we never read about a solution. No prescriptions or plans seem to make life any different for native or foreign women who find themselves in these circumstances. The book makes no overt cry for change in society, no call for justice. Ruth doesn't lead the charge for a change in situations for unattached women.

I wonder: Would you and I welcome Ruth today? As North American Christians we must continue to ponder how this book might speak to our modern-day issues surrounding immigration, race, language, or cultural distinctions.

This book of the Bible ends with high praises for Ruth. She is hailed as being worth more than seven sons to Naomi (Ruth 4:15). In spite of that high praise, Ruth is still remembered as Ruth *the Moabitess*. Why not just call her Ruth? The New Testament refers to her simply as Ruth (Mt. 1:5) and offers her higher praise still by including her in the genealogy of Jesus. But how might we remember Ruth and her contributions in our world today?

 **He Said**

I'm impressed with Boaz because he opens his heart to the foreigner in the land. He didn't have to welcome Ruth—this Moabite woman— but he did. He didn't have to make his lands available to those from "beyond the border." But he did. And he certainly didn't have to marry Ruth; she was the wrong nationality. But he married her nonetheless.

I wonder how these themes play out in our nation. We who, in this great land, hold up a beacon through the Statue of Liberty and proclaim, "Give me your tired, your poor, your huddled masses"? Is there a Boaz in us? These are large questions for our modern world with social, economic, and theological implications.

Closer to home—is our church open to the stranger, the foreigner, the alien in the land? Are our congregations welcome centers or walled fortresses? In short, do we demonstrate hospitality?

Boaz was hospitable. We cannot truly appreciate the sins associated with inhospitality during his day. The prophets spoke to the atrocities of not caring for the widow, the orphan, and the alien with uncompromised fervor. It's the open heart and the open hand that God desires.

Some years ago, I learned a great deal about hospitality when I served a college campus congregation. I learned that, indeed, the church is often "home" to people from other lands. Many students looked to the church first, as a people who would welcome and encourage. I'm so glad that congregation showed this hospitality. I learned so much. It was a joy learning about other customs, cultures, and cuisine. My life experiences were broadened immeasurably and so were my faith and my heart.

Boaz became the great-great-grandfather of King David. And how? By opening his hand.

Simple. Yet profound.

 She Said

Ruth approached quietly, uncovered his feet and lay down.
—Ruth 3:7b (NIV)

My childhood was lived during the era of *The Brady Bunch*, *Eight Is Enough*, and other sitcoms featuring blended families. But no story about remarriage can match the clever wit and sexually provocative tale of Ruth and Boaz. I think Ruth might have taken a few lessons from the writer of the Song of Songs. She asserts herself in more than one way throughout the story, even spurring Boaz to move beyond passivity in response to her. Ruth is an unconventional woman living in exceptional circumstances.

Husbandless and childless in the country of Moab, Ruth clings to her mother-in-law, Naomi, and together they return to Naomi's fertile, harvest land of Bethlehem. While there, her kinswomen recognize Naomi, while shunning her daughter-in-law. (Only after she has a son, Obed, do the neighbor ladies even acknowledge Ruth's presence.)

The love story of Ruth and Boaz runs counter to most other biblical love stories. Typically, the man left home, sought his fortune, and then met his future bride—perhaps near the town well when the women came to draw water. In this Bible narrative, the gender roles are reversed.

Ruth leaves her home and seeks her fortune but experiences prejudice, famine, and difficulty. She initiates a conversation with Boaz's servant in charge of the reapers so that she may join the reapers. She goes to work in the field gleaning the harvest—an act signifying that she was poor and was reduced to eating the leftovers. While harvesting in the field, Boaz, the owner, notices her and inquires as to her presence. Her future husband offers Ruth a drink (Ruth 2:9–14).

Throughout their first encounter, sexual tension underlies the entire conversation. This is far more noticeable in the Hebrew than in our English translations. Ruth prostrates herself at Boaz's feet, acknowledges his generosity, and states she is not his servant and so does not deserve the kindness and hospitality he is showing her. Boaz repeatedly expresses concern for her safety among the men. Is this a hint that he is attracted to her?

My favorite line of text arrives in chapter 3, quoted at the beginning of this section. Here I need to pause and thank my Old Testament professor at Duke Divinity School, Dr. James "Mickey" Efird, for this insight into the text. I recall his lecture when he, with a clever wink, informed us that uncovering a man's feet and being under his cloak seem innocent enough, but in Hebrew the translation could be otherwise. Cloak or *kanap* could mean an outer garment but could also refer to a man's genitals. Now the story is even more titillating!

Ruth made a bold move to obtain security for herself and for Naomi through the Levirate law—a law that Boaz does later affirm and complete. He will become Ruth's husband and father children through her, as the law states.

Now here is an interesting turn of events. Ruth's story either warns readers that Gentile women like Ruth were sexually forward (and therefore dangerous) or the book commends Ruth for her exemplary moral loyalty to the ways of Naomi and Boaz's God. The latter is where the conclusion of the book takes us.

No matter whether Ruth is to be praised or criticized, one thread runs throughout the story. Even though Ruth asserted herself sexually—seeking and obtaining a mate and her future security—the story assumes conventional roles for men and women. In the age of the judges, a female's primary worth was based on producing sons. We hear this in Naomi's anguish after her husband and boys are killed (Ruth 1:20–21), and we see that this is how Naomi is praised and how Ruth is finally acknowledged—after she gives birth to Obed (Ruth 4:14). Her baby and his descendants—from David to Jesus— ultimately offer Ruth praise for her part in God's plan.

 ## He Said

So Boaz took Ruth and she became his wife. When they came together, the LORD made her conceive, and she bore a son . . . They named him Obed; he became the father of Jesse, the father of David.
—Ruth 4:13, 17b

In seminary I read Ruth in the original Hebrew and learned that some very playful elements are at work in the text. Ruth is one of those "go girls!" She does what she has to do to get her man.

Here she is—a stranger in a strange land—and her mother-in-law, Naomi, instructs her to go and see Boaz one evening after he has finished his dinner and drunk his fill of wine (Ruth 3:3). Finding Boaz passed out on the threshing floor, Ruth "uncovers his feet" (Ruth 3:7) while he is sleeping—an act that has some deep sexual undertones to it.

When Boaz wakes in the morning, he discovers Ruth lying at his "uncovered" feet and agrees that she is a woman of honor. He will, he promises, marry her if the next of kin doesn't fulfill his responsibility according to the Levitical law.

I appreciate this playful tidbit in Ruth—it shows me that she was intelligent, sly, and secure in herself. She wasn't going to wait around and see how life played out—she went out there and made her future. That says a lot about this first-millennium B.C. gal. She was the original Wonder Woman.

Still, I am also in awe of what many women accomplish—especially despite the odds. Women have to overcome more than men, generally. A successful woman is also a marvel.

I've known hundreds of successful women—and if I'm honest, I have to admit that I have been blessed by them. My mother was successful (she reared ME!). I have also been blessed by highly influential female teachers, by professors, by female pastors, colleagues, and friends.

Maybe Ruth got things going for women, I don't know. I'm glad Ruth's success wasn't just defined by money, prestige, or power. Rather, her success was defined by the heart, by motherhood, by marriage, and by posterity.

She was, after all, the great-great-grandmother of King David, who was the g-g-g-g-g-great-grandfather of Jesus, who is brother to us all. Way to go, Ruth!

Boaz also impresses me. What a man. Here was a fellow who had not only a large wallet, but a big heart. We learn from reading this little book that Boaz accepted Ruth even though she was a "foreigner" (Ruth 2:10), that he withheld nothing from her of his worldly goods (Ruth 2:15–16), and that he was a man of honor (Ruth 3:11–13).

We might say that Boaz's life was defined by generosity. He didn't just give a tip to God; he gave a tithe (10 percent). He was not content to fulfill the letter of the law by leaving the corners of his fields ungleaned (so the poor would have something to eat), but he assisted the poor in harvesting the best stands of his produce. Boaz wasn't self-centered; he was other-centered.

Every man can learn from Boaz. We might learn integrity, or determination, or generosity. We can also learn that God does bless the faithful or, as Jesus once noted, that God gives even more to those who are faithful over a little (Luke 19:17). Boaz is faithful, and God continues to bless him with even greater wealth, which Boaz redeems and gives away in return for even greater blessings.

Wow, what a lesson in generosity.

In our modern culture, with so much emphasis on obtaining stuff for our own use, or securing more for ourselves, Boaz serves as a refresher course in faithful giving. He's a great role model, someone who can help us to understand how tithing to God's work offers up even greater rewards.

So often, we give God the leftovers of our work instead of the first fruits. Or perhaps we take most of God's blessings for ourselves and only give back a small tidbit of God's abundance to help the less fortunate. Or perhaps we don't even consider such things at all but just go through life taking, and taking, and taking without giving anything at all to God's work.

I'm glad Boaz is in the Bible. He's a model of masculinity.

Discussion and Reflection

1. All of us have unconventional relationships in our family tree. Share how those relationships brought a gift or a blessing to your family that would not have been there otherwise.

2. How can we honor Ruth's story today by acting justly toward others—especially those who immigrate to our land?

3. Talk about men in your life who have modeled Boaz-like generosity.

4. Tell stories about women you've known who were Ruth-like in their power and success.

5. What blessings have you received from choosing to "open your hand" to another who was in need?

6. The lineage of Jesus is traced back to Ruth. How is Ruth significant to the gospel message?

Chapter 7

Lovers in the Song of Songs
The Song of Songs

From the time the Song of Songs was included in the Jewish and Christian canon (the scriptures), the book has presented particular challenges to readers and interpreters. For more than a millennium of Jewish and Christian history, the book was allegorized heavily or thought to have symbolic or spiritual meaning—since most people couldn't bear the thought that this biblical book might actually be about the obvious: love and sex.

An early church theologian named Origen (185–254) so heavily allegorized the book that he gave it three levels of meaning. He saw it as a love poem, an allegory about Christ and his church (the bride), and a symbolic journey of the soul toward God. Nearly a thousand years later, Bernard of Clairvaux (1090–1153) epitomized this continuing allegorical approach and actually preached eighty-six sermons about this book, each message revealing a different interpretation of the Song's meaning.

For long spells of Christian history, the church withheld this scroll from young eyes until youth had been confirmed or were able to handle its "hot" contents. Regardless of the many attempts to look past the obvious, in the Song of Songs or the Song of Solomon we have a sex book in the Bible.

Why not? The Bible is replete with stories about people "knowing" each other and "begetting" children. Even if for some reason we don't regard sex as a fit subject for church, the fact remains, since creation sex has been God's chosen method of birthing us into the world!

So . . . why don't we talk more about sex—healthy sex and sexuality, love and loving—in the context of the Bible? After all, we can find plenty of love and sex in the pages of God's book.

So go ahead. Peek.

Take a look at the Song of Songs.

 # She Said

Place me like a seal over your heart,
like a seal on your arm;
for love is as strong as death,
its jealousy unyielding as the grave.

—Song of Songs 8:6a (NIV)

In my years of pastoral ministry I am surprised that only one couple has chosen a passage from Song of Songs for their wedding. I find it odd—but mostly I find it disappointing. Song of Songs is a fantastic book! It should be read and reread more often in the church. Love, sex, and romance are all in here. Why don't these couples see Song of Songs' potential—not only for their weddings but for their marriages, too? Why don't they read portions to each other over candlelight? Or email or text verses to one another as little love poems?

My frustration is further deepened by the reality that I, along with many other pastor colleagues, will readily admit our dislike for presiding over weddings. I'm not the only pastor who would rather preside over a funeral every week instead of helping a couple sort through their raging hormones, plan their extravagant reception, order their frilly flowers and expensive dresses, and deal with crazed mothers. Whew—weddings are exhausting. It is helpful for me to remember that funerals do have the word "fun" in them. But this is not always the pastor's experience when it comes to weddings. As I guide couples through their wedding and marriage preparations, I give them homework, asking them to read their Bibles. The idea of scriptural homework may be shocking to some people, but I do it anyway. My *United Methodist Book of Worship* lists a host of suggested scripture texts from both the Old Testament and the New Testament that are appropriate readings for wedding services. I ask couples to sort through this list and choose a scripture that reflects their thoughts on God, Christian marriage, and their unique relationship. I tell them to make a "date night" and read the Bible together.

Interestingly enough, one selection from the Song of Solomon (2:10–14, 16a and 8:6–7) is listed as a second choice on this long list of scripture readings but is rarely chosen by a bride and groom.

The most common wedding scripture has to be Paul's letter to the church in Corinth, chapter 13—a passage that was never intended for the mushy romance love of a couple, but was written to define the *agape* love for a community of faith. Now, don't get me wrong: 1 Corinthians 13 isn't a poor choice, but rather it just seems inconsistent with all of our wedding and premarital issues, cultural trends, and our ideas about romantic love.

I am really amazed at what couples miss out on by not selecting a passage from this steamy biblical love song. Songs of Songs contains the most titillating and romantic speeches by a woman and her suitor. This book has a more mature rating than G or PG!

My frustration is further compounded when many couples want secular love songs sung at their wedding services—songs that are highly influenced by hormones and the early stages of romantic feeling. Yet many couples shy away from these expressions of biblical romance, unconditional love, and great sex. What a shame—because this book provides great examples of healthy foreplay and gives sexuality a good name!

Aren't you glad that the great church of the past decided to include this book in the canon? I am. Because we would be missing out on so much if Song of Songs was just an abandoned scroll in a cave. It is too bad that portions of Song of Songs don't ever appear in the Protestant or Roman Catholic lectionaries (the three-year cycle of biblical texts as a guide for reading and preaching in worship). If we read more from this book, I think worship attendance might actually increase!

 # He Said

Let him kiss me with the kisses of his mouth!

—Song of Songs 1:2

Your two breasts are like two fawns,
  twins of a gazelle
  that feed among the lilies.

—Song of Songs 4:5

Americans have always had an odd fascination with, and approach to, sex. We typically don't discuss sex, although our culture is saturated with sexual images, scantily clothed models, and heaping doses of internet pornography, Hollywood movies, and sexually charged television sitcoms. We act as if we are not affected by sex, although we know that sex sells everything from hamburgers to automobiles. We don't want to give our children and teenagers healthy information about sex, although the teen pregnancy rate in the United States ranks among the highest in the world. We tell sexual jokes, but we are offended by frank sexual discussions in the classroom. We don't talk about sex in church, even though there is more sex mentioned in the Bible than we care to admit. In short, we are confused about sex—or, at least, we don't know how to discuss it.

But then, maybe human beings have always been confused about sex.

Let's take our lovers in the Song of Songs. Here they are, showing up in the middle of the Bible, speaking about love, kisses, and soft couches and talking about lips and breasts and the plans they have for the weekend. They speak of dreaming, undressing each other, and a thousand beautiful nights. More than a few people out there blush when they read this sexually charged love poem.

This is a love poem! A beautiful one at that. It has truth and grit, honesty and passion—all the stuff that great love stories and great relationships should have. It has all the wonderful words and phrases that women love to hear. As a man, I can appreciate the fact that this poem is in the Bible. After all, men need a few great poems that we can tap from time to time, since most of us can't write or express our feelings very well. We need the Shakespeares and the Wordsworths and the Audens to help us express what we want to say. That's why this poem is in the Bible! Men need the help.

Let's be honest. Women don't have as much trouble reading the Song of Songs as we men do. It's a fact. Who is buying all of those romance novels? Not men! Women love sweet talk and honesty—and the Song of Songs delivers this in a big way.

Personally, I think every man should read the Song of Songs and take some tips from it. We need to be more expressive in our love. We can't just show love . . . we have to say "I love you," too.

 ## She Said

How handsome you are, my lover!
Oh, how charming!
And our bed is verdant.

—Song of Songs 1:16 (NIV)

Many readers are shocked, astonished, or dumbfounded by the sexually provocative writing that they discover tucked between Ecclesiastes and the prophet Isaiah. This astonishment is further heightened when readers find that God is never mentioned in this book. Esther and Song of Songs have this in common, and yet the book of Esther does presume worship and prayer as a part of that narrative. Song of Songs, on the other hand, is often regarded by moderns as the most unsacred book, or the most secular book, in the Bible.

Then again, what is sacred, and what is secular? What is more sacred than love, intimacy, passion, and affection? All the talk show gurus, magazine writers, and therapists tell us that sex is best when it is anticipated, longed for, and appreciated in a mutual loving relationship. The Bible says so too, folks. All of these images come alive as the beloved pines for her lover in Song of Songs.

That is right I wrote *her* lover. While the sexual imagery and connotations in this book receive at least a PG-13 rating, what is most intriguing and exciting to me is the protagonist of this song. She is a she. A woman's voice sings much of this love song. She is one of a kind in the library of biblical books.

No one else talks for this woman. She has her own voice. Her voice is a voice recorded and included in a world where only tenors, baritones, and basses had the right to sing. Many scholars agree that in all likelihood the author of this book was a woman—perhaps one of Solomon's wives, but not Solomon himself, as tradition claims.

Maybe, just maybe, a soprano or alto voice does make a big difference. Maybe that is why Song of Songs is also the only place in scripture in which the Bible does not put rules, prohibitions, and restrictions around sex and sexuality—especially female sexuality. So much of what we read either in the Old or New Testament wrap the conversation about sexuality within the mandate of law. "Do this" and "do not do this" is the most common sexual conversation found in the Bible. Sex is certainly included in the Top Ten (that is, in the Ten Commandments).

In the Song of Songs we find a book that creatively explores and freely delights in sexuality. It is a wonderland for the lover and beloved to play together and explore each other! No restrictions, just wonder and awe regarding each other. While the metaphors for beauty and love seem a bit outdated, these two lovers delight in each other's taste (4:11), touch (7:8–9), smell (4:16), and the sound of the other's voice (5:16). Thus this unique book of biblical literature has a very special social and theological contribution to make to the whole of sacred scripture for Jews and Christians!

Please do not misread my thoughts and intentions here. I am not proclaiming that Song of Songs is the Hebrew and Christian equivalent of the Kama Sutra (an ancient Indian text widely considered to be the standard work on human sexual behavior). The Kama Sutra does contain practical advice on the act of sex and by some folks' standards is considered pornographic in nature.

I would argue that, while the Song of Songs comes closest to representing erotic literature as a genre, this book certainly offers more than just satisfying physical sensations or sexual release. Erotic writing in the Song of Songs links the physical gratification of sexuality with the deep emotions of a person's innermost thoughts and feelings. In simple terms, this erotic literature is sensual and connects acts with feelings. As far at the Bible goes, this is the book couples can enjoy together.

 # He Said

As I consider the Song of Songs on a deeper level, I discover that these lovers were more than just expressive. They were one. Isn't that what the scriptures teach us about marriage? Genesis 2:24 states that "therefore, a man leaves his father and mother and clings to his wife, and they become one flesh." Later, the apostle Paul would call this unity of the flesh "a great mystery" (Eph. 5:32).

Often, when we read about this unity, we forget that it is a fleshy togetherness. Marriage is about being one in mind and spirit, but it is also about being one in the flesh. The body, indeed all the parts of the body, is part and parcel of the intimacy of marriage. As far as I know, only my doctor and my wife have seen certain parts of my body. Some parts I have shared only with my wife. Likewise, my wife has shared herself with me. We are one in body. We are one in the flesh. As Paul said, "This is a mystery" that reveals the very heart of God and the meaning of the Christ's love for the church.

You see, Christianity has always been a faith of the flesh, of the body. That is why the first Christians insisted that Jesus was born "in the flesh" (he was not just a spiritual apparition) and why they insisted that Jesus actually suffered in the body, that he died a death on the cross, and that he was raised from the dead.

Early in church history many opposition movements countered these very "bodily" or "fleshy" ideas. Some could not stomach the idea of incarnation—that God took on the form of a servant and ate and drank with sinners. Rather, they held out various counterbeliefs, such as the doctrine that Christ didn't really suffer, that Christ didn't really die, or that Christ only seemed to eat and drink but was nothing more than a spiritual being who appeared to be human.

Reading the Song of Songs, I am reminded that our faith is very much tied to this body. In fact, the broad sweep of the Bible would seem to indicate that *we are bodies*. We don't just live in a body—the very essence of our existence is body.

When I read the Song of Songs, I celebrate God's creative work in the flesh. Kissing, hugging, and sex are very much a part of this fleshy unity between husband and wife. It's not just what a man and woman say to each other that matters . . . but what they do with each other, too. That's why the church has always insisted that there are healthy and biblical expressions of sex as well as unhealthy expressions. What we *do* matters. Our sexuality is a gift of God—and we are called to use our bodies to bless and affirm each other in love.

I like the Song of Songs. It's the best love poem I've ever read.

DISCUSSION AND REFLECTION

1. What is your definition of good sex? What formed that definition for you?

2. What can we gain from Song of Songs' understanding of sexuality and sensuality? Talk about how we can share or model that understanding with the children or teenagers in our lives.

3. What do you believe are differences between erotic and pornographic literature?

4. Have you ever written a love poem to someone you love? A love letter? Given a love gift in words? Explain.

5. What do you understand to be the connection between sexuality and sensuality?

6. What connections do you see between meaningful touch and the presence of God?

Chapter 8

Esther and Haman

The Book of Esther

The book of Esther joins the Song of Songs in never mentioning God. This characteristic was so obvious that later writers added verses to the book attributing leadership and answered prayer to God creating a book in the Apocrypha. In either version, Esther is a gloriously faith-filled story.

Movies such as *The King and I*, or more recently, *A Night with the King*, employ the themes of Esther, and even classic books like *1001 Arabian Nights* take some of their pizzazz and harem luster from this biblical book. This is more than a story about your average harem girl who catches the king's eye and later becomes queen. This is a story that speaks as much to our time—and in our time—as any biblical book. Here we find a story as old as time itself: hatred, ethnic cleansing, the threat of holocaust. God uses a humble Jewish woman, Esther, to save the Jewish people and reestablish the ancient customs of Purim.

Esther speaks loudly in our day—not just for the Jew, but also for the Christian.

 She Said

"If it pleases the king," replied Esther, "let the king, together with Haman, come today to a banquet I have prepared for him."

—Esther 5:4 (NIV)

What a pair of contenders Haman and Esther make! Archrivals locked in a social, religious, and political battle of wills, each is focused on survival and victory. You can almost hear the boxing announcer yell, "And in this corner weighing a slim 124 pounds dressed in a flowing chiffon gown and high heels we have Esther—beauty contest winner and queen! In the opposite corner her opponent, weighing in at a meaty 240 pounds without his armor, Haman—our military commander and the vizier to the king!" The bell rings, and the boxing match begins. In this biblical match, more is at stake than a fancy gold belt or a heavyweight championship title.

Esther wisely keeps her heritage and religion a secret from everyone—especially her opponent. Haman is actually a descendant of the Amalekites (Ex. 17:14–26), long-time adversaries of the Jews. Thus the battle set in this story is not just about two people throwing jabs at each other, but about a long-standing animosity between two peoples.

Haman and Esther, at first glance, seem like complete opposites: a brawny man versus a delicate beauty queen. Yet both Esther and Haman use what they have—their positions, good looks, relationship to the king, and cleverness—to get what they want. They are actually very similar in that respect. Their similarities make one wonder if— had it not been for the long-standing struggle between their peoples— Haman and Esther could have been friends instead of adversaries?

Even though these two have some things in common, they approach life very differently. Haman expects and demands that everyone will worship him: "When Haman saw that Mordecai would not kneel down or pay him honor, he was enraged" (Est. 3:5 NIV). Haman for all his ruthlessness is not a very smart man. He gets lulled into complacency and a sense of entitlement. His actions and attitudes reveal how small our enemies can be in terms of their character and bullish ways.

Esther uses both her beauty and her queenly assets to help others: "Esther answered, 'I and my people have been sold for destruction and slaughter and annihilation'" (Est. 7:4a NIV). Who could know that a beauty contestant winner would become the savior of a people? Only God!

There are striking differences between Esther and Haman and the legacies they wish to leave behind. Haman wants people to applaud him, laud him, and praise him. Esther desires what is best for her people and risks her life to obtain the legacy of her community's survival. Thus we have a sharp contrast between selfish desires and unselfish desires. What might this story have to say about the legacy each of us desires to leave behind?

 ## He Said

As the Jew Mordecai and Queen Esther enjoined on the Jews, just as they had laid down for themselves and for their descendants regulations concerning their fasts and their lamentations. The command of Queen Esther fixed these practices of Purim, and it was recorded in writing.

—Esther 9:31b–32

Many men feel threatened by a woman who is intelligent, beautiful, and powerful: the holy trinity of ultimate femininity. I know I do. But that's why I married my wife . . . so I wouldn't have to worry about finding a woman like this. Only thing missing from her arsenal is wealth. The Bible is replete with women who possess these qualities. How about Sarah, Rebekah, Ruth—and certainly, Esther? Especially Esther!

Here's a woman who has it all going on. She's beautiful enough to get into the harem club, but she's also a woman of superior intellect, able to outwit all the men around her. In the end, she becomes rich and powerful, too—a full-fledged queen.

On the one hand, when I read Esther, I see the king of Persia in the foreground with Haman, the evil one, lurking in the shadows. On the other hand the crowned one and his chief advisor are merely pawns in a drama played out through the faithfulness of Esther. From the first page we know this woman is going to save everyone and make a few men look rather foolish along the way.

But I like her.

Still, the question hovers in the air—why do men feel threatened by women like her? It's a question for the ages. Esther had resolve. She was strong. Esther is a hero, however, not because of her qualities, but because she was faithful to God. Often, when you and I think of faith, we think of folded hands and whispered prayers, but the book of Esther gives us another snapshot of the faithful life. Here we discover that faith can also be strategy, trust in the face of overwhelming odds, a quick wit, and resolve to deliver others who are in danger.

When I think of Esther I also think of other faithful ones who must live in very difficult circumstances. Teachers in our inner cities come to mind. Social workers who help others navigate through a maze of poverty and red tape. Diplomats who are working behind the scenes to bring about a more peaceful world.

Our faithfulness matters, too—yours and mine.

In our difficulties, we often discover that God can take us from a place of hardship into a place of blessing and honor. Not all difficulties end in tragedy. Like Esther, some of our struggles end in triumph.

 # She Said

Then Queen Esther answered, "If I have found favor with you,
O king, and if it pleases your majesty, grant me my life—this is
my petition. And spare my people—this is my request."
—Esther 7:3 (NIV)

I have never met a person —male or female—who enjoys or relishes being powerless. No one desires this experience, and yet history is replete with human oppression and one people subjugating another.

In the book of Esther, we encounter a people held captive by the larger political and cultural force called Persia. Not only did the Jewish people not have a vote, they were captives in a foreign land and had no voice to influence public policy or attitude.

The book of Lamentations, perhaps, captures this voice of the helpless, where people cried out against tyranny: "For these things I weep; my eyes flow with tears; for a comforter is far from me, one to revive my courage; my children are desolate, for the enemy has prevailed" (Lam. 1:16).

Imagine the power of Esther's witness during the Jewish diaspora in the days of the Persian Empire! Her life becomes a type of parable for what the Jewish people are experiencing. In the book of Esther we see a person (and consequently, a people) who has been dropped into a foreign land, but unexpectedly enters a place of power—the royal palace itself. The fact that Esther is both young and female accentuates her lack of power and her inability to defend herself. Esther is, in essence, the epitome of a diaspora Jew.

Moreover, we learn that Esther's opportunity for power as the next-in-line candidate for queen is precarious. After all, the king treated his previous queen badly. Queen Vashti was a very strong female who refused to come at the king's bidding and appear before his intoxicated nobles at a party. Her refusal was viewed by both King Ahasuerus and his courtiers as a threat to the order of things between husbands and wives. Vashti's disobedience had social, political, and economic ramifications. Her punishment, ironically enough, was what she wanted all along. She is banished from the kingdom no longer to be seen by the king!

Exit Vashti. Enter Esther. In spite of her helpless position, Esther is able to maneuver her way through the Persian courts of power. She wins the favor of the harem leader—a eunuch named Hegai. Hegai slates Esther for special spa treatments and gives her the top place in the harem. From there, Esther continues to use her own assets while receiving wise counsel from both her uncle and from Hegai. They train Esther well. She wins the favor of the king (Est. 2:17).

Through her position and her clever maneuvering of the King's emotional state, Esther prevents the genocide of her people. I wish that stopping genocide could be as simple and clear-cut today as it was in Esther's time. Modern tales of genocide from places like Armenia or the European Holocaust during World War II or Cambodia, Bosnia, Rwanda, and Darfur are incredibly complex and difficult to resolve. Could one young woman have this impact in our day, I wonder?

During the winter of 1993 I traveled to Israel with a group from my home congregation. One highlight of the tour was the Holocaust Museum in Jerusalem. In my teen years *The Diary of Anne Frank* was a favorite book of mine. During college, the writings of Dietrich Bonhoeffer became my new favorite. Even though I had read these works and had taken many history classes, I was unprepared for the impact the Holocaust Museum had on me.

Especially impactful was the landscaped walkway that led to the museum's entrance. Carefully pruned along the sidewalk path were trees planted in honor and memory of all those friends who rescued, hid, saved, fought for, and liberated Jews during World War II. Bronze plaques honored their names, nationalities, and ways in which these friends helped to make a difference.

As I consider the book of Esther, I wonder if this story might encourage and rally people today. I wonder where we might plant a tree for Esther and for all of those who work today to save lives.

 ## He Said

The past century has been littered with genocide of horrific proportions. Both World Wars produced massive loss of human life in addition to the Jewish Holocaust itself. We have also seen the killing fields of Cambodia. In more recent times, we have seen renewed attempts to exterminate entire peoples. Ethnic cleansing is the new phrase—and it has reared its ugly head in Rwanda, Iraq, and Pakistan, among other places.

In the book of Esther, Haman represents more than just a man. He represents an ideology that has been a part of the human struggle for centuries. It is hatred poured out—not from one person upon another—but through mass extermination.

Esther makes me wonder: Could women do a better job than men at ending this madness? God knows, men haven't produced much in the way of results on this front. But here is Esther, saving an entire people.

Recently I read a story about a modern-day Esther, a very real story about a woman named Maggie who lives in Burundi. Maggie, a devout Catholic, began her work by adopting children. When tribal leaders showed up with weapons, demanding that Maggie tell them if these children were Hutu or Tutsi, she refused, simply telling the soldiers they were all children of God. The soldiers made Maggie watch as they massacred more than seventy people. She later found her adopted children hiding in the food pantry in the town church.

Maggie migrated to a local village and renamed it Shalom (Peace). She converted a mass grave into a town swimming pool and renovated another building into a movie theatre. Her reasons? "Children need to know that there are beautiful experiences in the world and laughter," she said. "Life is not about death." Over the years, Maggie adopted dozens of children, including one young man who came into the village to murder her. "You can kill me," she told him, "but you will never find fulfillment spending your life in hiding in the bush." He stayed in the village, and she became his mother.

Are there still modern-day Esthers? I think so. Faith is still a powerful force. So is love.

Just ask Maggie.

DISCUSSION AND REFLECTION

1. Name contemporary people or some from past history who were motivated by their own gain (like Haman). Create another list of people motivated by their desire to help others. Which list would you prefer to be on some day? Why or why not?

2. How can one woman (or one man) save a people today?

3. Do you agree or disagree that men are threatened by intelligent, beautiful, or powerful women? Why or why not?

4. How might we model faith more powerfully through action rather than through worship and prayer?

5. How would the world be different if women led instead of men? In government? In business? In communities?

6. What lessons have you learned from someone in a position of power?

Chapter 9

Women and Men
at the Empty Tomb

Matthew 28 and Luke 24

Each of the four gospels (Matthew, Mark, Luke, and John) has a "resurrection narrative"—that portion of the gospel devoted to the hours and days following the crucifixion of Jesus. These narratives do vary and reveal, in part, the particular perspectives of the gospel writers.

Matthew, for example, gives us women at the empty tomb, an angel's appearance, and the proclamation that Jesus will meet the disciples in Galilee. The final four verses of this gospel emphasize Jesus telling the disciples to "go into all the world."

In contrast, Mark's gospel, in its oldest and shortest version, has no resurrection appearance, but women receive an angel proclamation of resurrection at an empty tomb.

Then, Luke's gospel features the women at an empty tomb, an angel proclamation, and then later several appearances of the risen Christ, including an appearance near Emmaus and a subsequent appearance that sends the apostles back to Jerusalem.

Finally, John's gospel features women at the empty tomb followed by an array of resurrection appearances, including a private Christ appearance to Mary, a Christ appearance to ten of the apostles followed by another with Thomas present, and a Christ appearance on the shore of the Sea of Galilee.

What do all of these gospel narratives have in common? Just one thing: the women were the first to visit the empty tomb and receive the good news. Let's have a closer look at what this means.

 She Said

So the women hurried away from the tomb, afraid yet filled with joy, and ran to tell his disciples.
—Matthew 28:8 (NIV)

When I was growing up, I often visited my grandparents during the Easter holidays. Their small country congregation would join with others in their community for an Easter sunrise service held at the local high school gym. I don't know which I enjoyed more: being with my favorite grandparents; wearing my new Easter dress; enjoying the sunrise Easter service that included, afterwards, a buffet of breakfast goodies; or hearing a story about Jesus where women were the primary witnesses!

I hope my fondness for Easter has more to do with a deep theological understanding of what resurrection means than these tidbits, but I am not so sure that some of my fond feelings aren't influenced by the fact that Easter, like Christmas, has a primary "girl part" in it. So many Old Testament dramas (and New Testament stories too) include plenty of great roles for boys. The Easter narrative has strong female leads.

Often when I am questioned both personally and professionally about my calling as a female into ordained ministry, I return to the Easter stories of my childhood faith. The girls were not just "there" at the empty tomb, I remind my opposition. The women in the gospels of Matthew, Mark, and John were given a commission to "go and tell"! And that's what they did. The ladies who came to the tomb that Easter morning were technically the first to evangelize. That is, they were the first to share the good news of Jesus' death and resurrection with others. We should remember: women and men are equally enlisted into the service of sharing this good news. If the women were perfect for God's purposes on the first Easter, then God still calls capable women to preach, teach, and evangelize today in our churches, communities, and mission fields around the world and here at home.

Long ago as a music therapy intern in Oklahoma, I met a tall Texas rancher with an even taller mustache. Somehow this weather-worn man found out about my acceptance to seminary and wanted to talk with me. As he sauntered over in his dusty, red cowboy boots, I was uncertain how our conversation would proceed. I was stunned when he said with a deep Texan accent, "Little lady, I just don't see why women can't be preachers. You gals birth us into life—why not birth us into our eternal life too?"

My cowboy advocate remembered rightly that a girl child named Mary was chosen by God to bear God's Son into the world. Why wouldn't God choose a second Mary (as in Mary Magdalene and the other Mary) to "bear the Good News" into the world? Why wouldn't God enlist all God's children in telling and retelling the greatest story ever told!? God needs the help of all humanity because we know "the harvest is plentiful, but the workers are few" (Mt. 9:37 NIV).

 **He Said**

And returning from the tomb, they [the women] told all this to the eleven and to all the rest. Now it was Mary Magdalene, Joanna, Mary the mother of James, and the other women with them who told this to the apostles. But these words seemed to them an idle tale, and they did not believe them. But Peter got up and ran to the tomb; stooping and looking in, he saw the linen cloths by themselves; then he went home, amazed at what had happened.

—Luke 24:9–12

In the first-century Jewish world, women didn't have much clout as witnesses. Two or more were required to give valid testimony—especially against a man. The testimony of only one woman was dismissed. This fact looms large in the resurrection narratives in each of the gospels. After all, a group of women, and not a group of men, first heard the good news that Jesus had been raised from the dead.

Whenever I read the resurrection accounts, I am moved by the willingness of the women to return to the men and proclaim the good news. Certainly, the women knew they would face masculine resistance. Their faith in carrying out the mission is a powerful testimony even today.

Of course, we moderns are slow to accept anything that cannot be explained rationally. In our day, it is equally incredible to accept that someone could rise from the dead. On the other hand we live in a time when people will believe almost anything. There are more cults today than ever before. Leaders who proclaim wild, absurd, and monstrous ideas (even violent and extremist ideas) seem to get their share of followers. At times, it even seems that claims now have to be even more bizarre to gain the attention of would-be disciples.

What might these modern-day ideologies have to tell us about the power of the resurrection of Jesus—which is, after all, good news?

 # She Said

But the apostles didn't believe a word of it, thought they were making it all up.

—Luke 24:11 (The Message)

We should not be surprised to learn that the men did not believe the women's story about a conversation with an angel and an empty tomb. The women brought news that seemed to come from the bizarre end of the spectrum. The male disciples were not prepared to receive or believe such news. We must give the men some slack for their disbelief. After all, resurrection was something new and radical. We have a tough time believing it today.

Likewise, we should not be flabbergasted by the men's slowness to accept the women's message—for they were, after all, *women* who followed Jesus. In first-century Judea, women were not allowed to testify in legal matters, and a woman's word was not given much weight.

Some would argue that it would have been better for the gospel if the men had heard the good news first. But the truth is, the ladies got there first. This inclusion of the women, however, provides historicity to the resurrection narratives. The gospel writers were more concerned with being faithful—even if the details proved embarrassing—than they were about recasting the story to make it more acceptable within the cultural norms. It is strangely ironic, I think, that a patriarchal society would base the acceptance of the gospel message upon a woman's testimony. Such unbelievable, anticultural testimony from normally discredited messengers lends strong credence to the reality and truthfulness of the gospel story. Herein is another example that God can use everyone to achieve God's purposes.

What can you and I as modern disciples take away from this rift between the Easter testimony of the men and women? Does this encounter point to an archetypal disagreement between unbelieving, unfaithful men and believing, faithful women? Is this a New Testament battle of the sexes for proper faithfulness and belief? Or does it begin to heal such a gap between the sexes?

I believe none of these. Luke's Easter narrative simply does not provide enough evidence to point to a war between women who believe and men who do not believe. Luke is uninterested in this contrast. Nor does he try to blend the stories of the two gender groupings. Rather, the writer of Luke seems to be more interested in making the connection between a person's direct encounter with the risen Jesus and a person's newfound faith.

Later in Luke, we see this in the Emmaus story and the interlude about Thomas. These two later Easter stories focus on Jesus' risen appearance and the direct contact he had with male and female disciples. Gender is not an issue at all.

Think about it. All of us have had encounters with friends or family who do not believe our personal stories of faith. Some friends may roll their eyes when we mention how God has been at work in our lives. Family members—male or female—may doubt our sincerity at times. Disbelief changes to belief only when these loved ones have had their one-on-one direct encounter with the mystery of God. Then we find them running to us—hoping and trusting that we will believe their testimony.

 # He Said

One underlying theme pops up in almost all resurrection accounts. That theme is doubt. For example, the men doubt the women when they return with news of the empty tomb. Later, Thomas doubts. On the Emmaus road, the unnamed disciples doubt if they had, indeed, encountered Jesus or if it was all a dream. At the end of Matthew's gospel, doubt is mentioned when Jesus offers the great commission to take the gospel into all the world.

Why would the gospel writers spend so much time telling us about doubt—wouldn't they want others to believe? Yes—but that's precisely the point. We do doubt. Doubt is very much a part of the human experience, even the experience of the faithful.

Like the men who first heard the gospel from the women, we doubt good news or the promise of life or hope. We give up easily. Or we prefer to live under the ideology that we are in control of our days and our ends, that we can work our way up the ladder and eventually secure our future.

The resurrection gospel tells us that we should also doubt these ideas—ideas we have about ourselves, our control, or our belief that we are in charge of our own destinies. The proclamation reminds us God is in control of life and death and life beyond death. We don't actually get to make the rules. God makes the rules and is remaking all of creation. And God can remake us, too.

That really is good news. Believe it?

 # She Said

When they heard that Jesus was alive and that she had seen him, they did not believe it.

—Mark 16:11 (NIV)

While I don't think that there is a gender battle in the Easter story, the contrast between men and women in the resurrection narratives does raise a question as to whether men and women express their spirituality differently. Are our different preferences in prayer practices, worship, and personal piety a mirror reflection of our gender—or of something else?

History is replete with evidence that the Western branch of the Christian church has long held onto traditional roles for women and men. Whether a church is Protestant or Roman Catholic, the male-dominated hierarchy is substantiated within church structure, polity, and access to leadership. My denomination for the last fifty years has opened leadership opportunities within the church for both women and men, yet pieces of the old structure and traditional roles still linger. While these traditional gender roles of "separate but equal" continue, another fascinating fact remains true. Female church members in both Catholic and Protestant churches (no matter their ethnic or socioeconomic background) make up more than half the people in the pew.

At a prayer gathering of women within my own congregation, the ladies lamented, "Where are all the men?" Their question was raised about the lack of men's ministry, small groups, and retreat ministry at our church, but the question could have been said about Sunday morning worship attendance as well.

Recently a variety of male Christian authors and writers has attempted to account for this lack of male presence in church. They advocate that men do indeed express their faith differently, just as women do. Some advocate that the differences are so vast that corporate worship on Sunday mornings in America no longer resonates with men. Some believe that men need to have life-changing adventure, or beat drums, or go on vision quests to connect their spirituality with God. Worship services have become, well—too girlish. Some advocate that worship is too weak, quiet, and unengaging to attract men today.

These ideas puzzle me. Why? Because most of the traditions centered around Christian worship have been written, articulated, managed, and handed down by men, for men, and with other men. So, what has happened? Have men changed? Have women changed? Or neither?

My questions remind me of a lunch conversation I had with a male colleague who said, "Female pastors are out to 'emasculate men.'" He told me this with such a straight face that I recall choking on my soup. But I wonder—was there a deeper source for his concern? This idea came from a man who has long been an advocate for women in leadership and in ministry, and so I know his comment was not based on ill feelings toward women, or for their leadership, but must have come from a place where he felt threatened as a man.

This statement does cause me to wonder about the absence of men in worship. Has our style of worship emasculated men from being men? If so, who is to blame? Or can blame even be assigned? More importantly, what can we do about it?

DISCUSSION AND REFLECTION

1. Talk about a time when a loved one gave you grief for your faith in Jesus. What was this like for you?

2. Women can be evangelists whether they are ordained in ministry or sent into the mission field. Who are your faith mothers, aunts, sisters, or friends who told you the goods news of Jesus? What impact has their word had in your life?

3. What is your experience with male and female spirituality? Is it different or the same?

4. What do you consider to be the factors that account for a lack of male presence and a large female presence in worship?

5. Why do people find it difficult to believe in resurrection today?

6. How are doubt and faith related in your experience with Jesus?

Chapter 10

Rhoda and Peter

Acts 12

The book of Acts is the second part of Luke's gospel. Acts offers a sneak peek into the early church, including insights into the development of leaders such as Peter. Acts also depicts the various trials and tribulations of the apostles, their work, and the growth of the church.

In the opening chapters of the book of Acts, Peter emerges as the premier leader of the church, with Paul (formerly Saul) beginning to take center stage after chapter 9 when he encounters the risen Christ on the road leading to Damascus. Chapter 12 presents a most fascinating story about the imprisonment of Peter and his miraculous deliverance.

In all this mix we also find a bit of humor, but the book of Acts is primarily a book about the church and the holy friendships that emerged to form the community of faith.

 ## He Said

When he [Peter] knocked at the outer gate, a maid named
Rhoda came to answer. On recognizing Peter's voice, she was

so overjoyed that, instead of opening the gate, she ran in and announced that Peter was standing at the gate. They said to her, "You are out of your mind!" But she insisted that it was so.

—Acts 12:13–15

This brief encounter between Peter and Rhoda actually has a deeper background and raises some intriguing questions about Peter. For example, Acts 12 recounts Peter's imprisonment at the hands of Herod. Herod has already killed James, the brother of John, and seemed intent to stamp out this small clan of Jesus people. So Herod arrests Peter. Right away, we begin to wonder: Will Peter be killed?

Peter is, imprisoned—cast into chains. His execution seems inevitable. Herod has set the date, and the clock is ticking. Enter an angel of the Lord, stage right. In his dark, grisly cell, Peter is suddenly surrounded by light, his chains are loosened, and he walks out of the jail. He hastens down a lane to the house of John Mark, where the church has gathered and is in deep prayer, hoping for Peter's release. Peter knocks at the gate. This brief episode has some punch to it. It is insightful and tells us much about Peter. First, I note that Peter is much different from the man at the end of Luke's gospel (the first half of the Luke-Acts narrative). The Peter of Acts is not the same Peter who denied Jesus in Herod's courtyard some months earlier. Peter is now bold, decisive, and faithful. He has grown into leadership and is willing to follow Christ along a path that Peter had earlier abandoned. The Acts jail story reveals a Peter who is now inspirational and exemplary. In short, Peter turned his life around. He turned his faith around. We can learn much from him.

We can benefit from Peter's example. It does no good to stay in a place of defeat and sorrow. Christ gives forgiveness and a new day. We don't have to linger in the shadows of failure when Christ has so much more for us to do—individually and collectively as a church. Peter kept moving. He embraced the leader within by trusting the Christ above.

I think of Peter especially during the tough times. Leadership is difficult even during the best of circumstances, but it is especially rough after a personal failure or when a crisis emerges. The Peter of Acts is a man of quality—a kingdom builder.

Anyone who would presume to lead today can learn much from him.

 She Said

Peter knocked at the outer entrance, and a servant girl named Rhoda came to answer the door.

—Acts 12:13 (NIV)

Even though stories about Peter abound in the New Testament, we can read about Rhoda only from this one brief episode in Acts. In this narrative we find Peter, a fisherman-turned-leader of the early church, seeking shelter after God sends an angel to rescue him from prison. Rhoda is a servant girl in John Mark's household, and she offers Peter hospitality. Now here is an unlikely pair, and yet Peter and Rhoda are yoked together in this story about ministry of the first-century church.

Because Rhoda was a slave and servant girl, her life was lived on the lowest rung of her culture. She served the whims of her owner—in this case, John Mark's mother. Luckily for Rhoda, her master was among the new followers of Jesus of Nazareth.

Peter, on the other hand, had quite a bit more stature. He was a tradesman in the fishing industry and was a leader in the Jesus movement. Despite these demographic and social differences, Peter and Rhoda had one thing in common: they were both servants sent on a mission.

Rhoda's mission was to care for the household of Mary (who just happened to accommodate the Jerusalem church in her home). Peter's mission was to serve Jesus' continuing legacy—the church. In this way both were servants of the church.

These servants bless us with some delightful humor and irony. Rhoda's humorous witness has the potential to remedy us from taking ourselves and our ministry in Jesus' name too seriously. First of all, how wonderfully upside-down for a woman to stand at the door to allow entrance to a convicted felon! Rhoda was in the unique position as both a servant and a female to hold the door open for Peter. Often, in our culture, men hold doors open for ladies, but here a woman holds the door open for a man. Rhoda does this because hospitality and the welcoming of a stranger or friend was an important part of Jewish life and would become a hallmark of the early church's ministry. In this scene Rhoda doesn't welcome a stranger per se but greets the very person everyone was waiting to meet. The guest of honor!

This encounter is reminiscent of another story in which the significance of knocking at a door is linked with prayer. Jesus used the image of knocking on a door to describe prayer to his disciples (Mt. 7:7–8; Luke 11:7–9). How ironic that the church people were praying for Peter at the same moment in which he knocked on the door! Jesus' lesson about prayer was fulfilled in the presence of the Jerusalem church as they prayed. Now I call that a teachable moment!

Before Rhoda welcomed Peter into the home, she shut the door in his face and rushed back into the home shouting the good news. I don't know about you, but I often burst out laughing at this point in the story. Can you not picture the odd look on Peter's face when the door is slammed shut and he hears nothing but shouting from inside the house? Too funny! Power brought Peter to the threshold of John Mark's home, and the power reverberated back and shut the door right back in his face. Rhoda was overwhelmed, startled, and totally thrown off course by his presence.

Rhoda's energetic door slam, shout inside the house, and rush to welcome Peter back remind me of a final story about Jesus and the door. John, the writer of Revelation, witnessed Jesus saying, "Here I am! I stand at the door and knock. If anyone hears my voice and opens the door, I will come in and eat with him, and he with me" (3:20 NIV).

On one level, Rhoda's reception of Peter at the door could be considered a means of welcoming Jesus. After all, Peter, a representative of Jesus' earthly church, was imprisoned because of his loyalty to Jesus. This causes me to wonder about those times in life when we may be startled by the powerful presence of Jesus standing outside the entry places of our lives. How often we do slam the door in his face?

 # He Said

This Bible story is humorous. Peter, weary from his imprisonment, his escape, and his long trek through the night, knocks at the gate of

John Mark's house. A young woman—who has been praying for Peter just moments earlier—opens the door and discovers that her prayers have been answered: It's Peter! In her excitement, she doesn't welcome Peter into the house. She runs back to the meeting and tells the others that their prayers have been answered. But, of course, they don't believe her. Who would? Meanwhile, Peter stands outside wondering if guards are chasing him.

This brief narrative is also one-half of the tradition that emerged about St. Peter, who not only held the keys of the kingdom, but also stood at the pearly gates of heaven to question those seeking admittance. Here's the first gate—and Peter is knocking on it.

The story of Rhoda and Peter is principally a story about prayer. Good things happen when people pray for each other. Sometimes, miraculous things happen.

In his slim volume, *Letters to Malcolm: Chiefly on Prayer*, C. S. Lewis described a personal experience of prayer this way:

> Last week, while at prayer, I suddenly discovered—or felt as if I did—that I had really forgiven someone I have been trying to forgive for over thirty years. Trying, and praying that I might. When the thing actually happened—my feeling was "But it's so easy. Why didn't you do it ages ago?"[1]

Many answers to prayer come suddenly and often surprise us. Perhaps we are praying for a family member, and then suddenly their problem dissolves—an answer to prayer. Or perhaps we pray for years to find an answer to a complex challenge in life, and the answer comes in stages. One day we realize, "That's it!"

When Rhoda opened the door, she realized that her prayers were answered, but she didn't know how to deal with the gift. She was amazed, shocked, awed. Why is it that we pray, but often doubt God's ability or willingness to transform and redeem?

---

1. Clive Staples Lewis, *Letters to Malcolm: Chiefly on Prayer* (New York: Harcourt Brace Jovanovich, 1963), 106.

 She Said

*But they wouldn't believe her, dismissing her, dismissing her
report. "You're crazy," they said. She stuck by her story, insisting.*
—Acts 12:15 (The Message)

The response of the church to Rhoda's announcement that Peter
stood at the door was the same reaction of the male disciples on Easter
morning: disbelief. Once again a female eyewitness relates what she has
seen and heard, and no one believes her. The church refuses to trust
her and in fact insists that she is delusional, seeing visions of Peter's
angel (Acts 12:15b). All of that sounds like a recasting of Luke 24.

Luke's aim in this, his historical journey of the church from
Jerusalem to Rome, tells the tale of Christianity's spreading beyond
the boundaries of a small Jewish sect into the larger, Gentile
world. Over half of the book is dedicated to Paul, and so all of the
personalities later seem to be playing second fiddle to Paul's robust
personality and his evangelism to Gentiles.

Moreover, information about women and their personal lives
tend to be at the periphery in this church narrative. Why? Luke
was a product of his time and culture and thus very interested in
proper leadership roles and social decorum. He desperately wanted
to appeal to his readers so that they too would hear his primary message about Jesus.

It is frustrating for modern disciples to catch a glimpse of the
early church when one half is so unevenly portrayed. How can we
appreciate our history and tradition when it reports so much disbelief
and mistrust in women's voices, theology, and personal piety? Church
history books reveal that female Christian mystics and theologians
like Hildegard of Bingen, Claire of Assisi, Mechthild of Magdeburg,
Julian of Norwich, Catherine of Siena, Margaret Kempe, Joan of
Arc, and Teresa of Avila were also not always heard or believed by
the church. These women each had their own "Rhoda moment"
when the church leaders did not believe them. We also have modern
"Rhodas" among us as well. Where does that leave church-going
women who are still not heard today?

I believe we can go back to Luke for assistance. Even though
he portrayed narrow views of women in his accounts, he never held

a narrow view of the powerful gospel of Jesus Christ. The gist of Luke's second volume of work is the unanimous attraction and influence of the good news of Jesus into the whole world—especially to Gentiles. Peter's vision of the clean and unclean animals—just two chapters prior to his experience with Rhoda—served as the epiphany moment when the "doors" were opened to all who wanted to believe in Jesus (see Acts 10). Barriers that had previously separated people were torn down by the message of Jesus. Following our story of Peter and Rhoda the entire book focuses more and more on Paul spreading the faith outward to all persons. When we apply Luke's theological understanding about Jesus' message to the recognition of women's voices within our faith, then we can see clearly women are no longer impure or unclean, but equals to their male counterparts.

 # He Said

Rhoda, in many ways, is the church. Surprised. Disbelieving. Incredulous. Still, she represents a community that offers more than prayer. They share hospitality, too. I think women appreciate the story of Peter and Rhoda more than men do. After all, the story of Peter's prison release ends at the doors of a home, with a welcome inside. Men can quickly dismiss the relationship between faith and home, but women seem to get this connection more readily. Hospitality is one of the key elements of the gospel.

When I consider how hospitality has shaped my faith, my experience of the church, I am astounded. When I was a student pastor in North Carolina, I frequently spent the night in people's homes. Each week, another family in the congregation would invite me to Saturday night dinner. We would eat, converse, and then they would show me to a guest room. The next morning, I would preach and teach. This type of hospitality went on for a couple of years—and I learned how personal and deep the faith is when hospitality is demonstrated. An open door and an open home are truly witnesses of Christ's love.

Men can show hospitality, too. How about at work, by taking a troubled coworker aside, or out to coffee, just to talk things over and show some caring, nonjudgmental support? Or how about after the workout, when a friend needs to talk over a problem? Or how about opening our homes to a member of the visiting choir or the missionary who is speaking at church? Men can have an impact by showing we care in many ways. Our hospitality doesn't have to be dainty or associated with matching hand towels. We can give gifts, or attach a new screen door, or tutor children, or visit the too-often-neglected senior citizens.

Hospitality, ultimately, isn't about the preparation. It's about opening the door.

DISCUSSION AND REFLECTION

1. Tell about a time when you or someone you know "shut the door on Jesus" due to surprise, excitement, or joy.

2. How might we be more accepting of those whose faith stories we have neglected or disbelieved?

3. Who in your life has been a "Peter"—a man of quality and a kingdom builder?

4. Tell of an experience when you were surprised by God's answ   .o your prayer.

5. What can your congregation do to offer a wider door of hos   tality to others?

6. How have you grown in your faith over time?

Chapter 11

Lydia and Paul

Acts 16

The book of Acts introduces us to various leaders in the early church, but none more influential that Paul. Acts turns personal when the narrative shifts from third-person to first-person narration. This shift occurs when Paul sets sail for the region of Macedonia and is obviously accompanied by Luke, the writer of the gospel of Luke and the Acts of the Apostles. In chapter 16, we also encounter Lydia, who turns out to be one of the most helpful women we will find anywhere in the Bible.

Paul's message of salvation is deliverance to Lydia and her household. Later, Lydia becomes an unexpected source of deliverance to Paul and his companions. It's an old-world story, but one that still resonates with truth and beauty.

 ## She Said

One of those listening was a woman named Lydia, a dealer in purple cloth from the city of Thyatira, who was a worshiper of God. The Lord opened her heart to respond to Paul's message.
—Acts 16:14 (NIV)

If conversing with women at a well was a good evangelism practice for Jesus (see John 4), then Paul put it into practice for his ministry by visiting women at the local river (see Acts 16). At the river bank he met Lydia, who was a Gentile, a single woman, and an entrepreneur. She eagerly responded to the message of Jesus, which was yet another sign and indication that the gospel was meant for Gentile hearers as well as Jews.

My fondness for the story of Lydia goes all the way back to my grade school days. My best friend in the world from kindergarten through second grade was named after this biblical woman. She too had an eagerness about her faith and lives her discipleship with and through her family today.

The story of Peter and Rhoda gives us a glimpse of women at the low end of the socioeconomic spectrum in first-century Judea. The story of Lydia offers us a glimpse into the lives of rich and powerful women—women who could influence the church through their economic status. Outside of Mary (Jesus' mother) and Rhoda, all other women mentioned in the book of Acts are wealthy, able to contribute financially to the work of the church. Luke wanted to show women in positions of influence.

Lydia was a businesswoman who specialized in luxury goods such as exclusive purple cloth. She was a leader in her community and within her home. I find it ironic that, out of all the people Paul could have met by a river, he found a woman who seemed perfectly content, but who also seemed perfectly content. Lydia had her entire household baptized with her (Acts 16:15), which is yet another indication of her status as well as her influence.

Paul encountered in Lydia an excellent match to his own strengths. They were both able and successful people of influence who were leaders and dealers in business (his was tent making, while hers was cloth and goods). Lydia becomes the first European Gentile convert, and her conversion parallels that of Peter and Cornelius in Acts 10. Due to Lydia's affluence and her access to the business world of Philippi (the community elite), Lydia becomes a formidable ally in the spread of Christianity. Acts 16:40 suggests that Lydia also opened up her home to Paul and Silas. Her home may very well have physically housed the local church community.

Paul's relationship with Lydia and her subsequent work with him and fellow believers provide us with a picture of the leadership roles both women and men occupied in the early church. You could describe Lydia's contributions to the Jesus movement as a benefactor or patron. Without her support, ministry would not have had the ability to care for the poor and widowed, nor would the work of traveling missionaries such as Paul, Silas, and others been supported as robustly.

Lydia is a model of generosity—and we can all learn much from her example.

 **He Said**

A certain woman named Lydia, a worshiper of God, was listening to us; she was from the city of Thyatira and a dealer in purple cloth. The Lord opened her heart to listen eagerly to what was said by Paul. When she and her household were baptized, she urged us, saying, "If you have judged me to be faithful in the Lord, come and stay at my home."

—Acts 16:14–15

When we consider our individual histories, I think we would all agree that certain defining moments have shaped and influenced us. Some of these defining experiences are choices we have made. Others are experiences we did not choose, but rather entered our lives unexpectedly. We have also made choices regarding location and timing that have shaped our lives significantly. Such choices lead us to people who often lead us to God.

That's how I see Paul's Macedonian decision. Convinced that God was calling him to share the good news with the people of Macedonia, he made a choice to travel to that region. And so he sailed. His decision was life-changing, not just for him, but for his companions and for the people he met. Paul's Macedonian experience became one of the defining moments of his life.

In the movie *Forrest Gump*, we encounter many larger-than-life characters whose decisions impact the world—though they don't often know it. Forrest's experiences as a young boy, his tour of duty in Vietnam, and his numerous introductions to sitting American presidents touch the lives of his beloved Jenny, his friends Bubba and Lieutenant Dan, and his mother. Each of them, in turn, affects others. The movie asks the question: Do we all have a destiny, or are we people who just float accidentally—as if on a breeze?

Reading Acts, we discover our decisions count for something. Taking one path as opposed to another can make all the difference in the world. Our choices of place, time, and people matter greatly. Paul's Macedonian decision influenced entire communities. Troas, Samothrace, Neapolis, Philippi, and Thyatira—these are just a few of the places and people this decision affected. We will concentrate on one woman and her family, in particular.

This narrative provokes us to question our own lives and motives. Am I in the right place at the right time? Where might God be calling me? Do I expect to hear God's voice?

 # She Said

"If you're confident that I'm in this with you and believe in the Master truly, come home with me and be my guests." We hesitated, but she wouldn't take no for an answer.
—Acts 16:15b (The Message)

Lydia's leadership role along with Paul's teaching and influence gives us a few more clues into the lifestyles of early church believers. Nothing indicates that Lydia ever left her business. It seems she continued her professional pursuits as she grew in her faith. Lydia, based upon the little we know about her, was able to integrate her faith with her business, and vice versa. Perhaps she found something in the ethics and teachings of Jesus that aided her in dealing fairly with customers as well as suppliers. It could have been that through her successful and sound business practices she was able to influence her colleagues to consider the truth about this Jesus of Nazareth. Who knows? We do know that many contemporary authors have explored the benefits of Jesus' teaching and ethics for the modern world of global and corporate economics.

Interestingly, wealth and status seem compatible with following Jesus even in the early church. So often in the gospel stories we see Jesus visiting with the marginalized and the poorest of the poor. Apparently, Jesus' own family was quite poor. The story of Lydia opens up access to all socio-economic groups who are touched and affected by Jesus' message. Sure, Jesus said, "It is easier for a camel to go through the eye of a needle than for a rich man to enter the kingdom of God" (Mt. 19:24 NIV). Jesus never said it was totally impossible, just difficult. He also said moments later regarding this same topic, "but with God all things are possible" (Mt. 19:26b NIV).

Because she had such a generous spirit in welcoming Paul and Silas into her home (and on more than one occasion), we must assume Lydia's generosity was expressed in other ways as well. She did not take no for an answer. Is she one of those Paul referred to in another letter as having the spiritual gift of giving? "We have gifts that differ according to the grace given us . . . the giver, in generosity" (Rom. 12:6, 8). Maybe Lydia was blessed with success *because* of her generosity and because her generosity blessed others through her success. Either way, the church under Paul and Lydia's leadership was able to flourish when other churches were having difficulty raising funds (see Phil. 4:15–16).

Just how much she was able to contribute to Paul's work is left unsaid in Acts. We do know that while in prison, Paul wrote to this church community with a great deal of affection and personal appreciation. He was especially thankful for their material (i.e., financial) support of his work (see Phil. 4:10–20). Lydia is never specifically named in this letter, but we can assume that her financial assistance was included in the total gift from the Philippian church. Who knows? Perhaps it was around her dining room table that this letter, the Epistle of Joy, was first read aloud to the Church of Philippi?

He Said

I like Lydia. She shows heart, determination, and a great capacity to love. We meet her in Philippi on a Jewish Sabbath. Paul and his companions walk a short distance outside the city to pray and encounter Lydia, who has come from Thyatira—a city known for its purple linens. She has come to Philippi, we assume, to sell her luxurious fabric. She has also come to worship.

When Paul explains the gospel to her, she becomes a believer in Jesus and requests that she and her entire "household" be baptized into the faith. Here, perhaps, we can assume that her husband and children were a part of this baptismal class—but we don't know for sure. Nevertheless, Lydia's faith is deep, and she invites Paul and his companions to stay at her house in Philippi.

Lydia's testimony has many dimensions to it. She is obviously of a wealthy class—as she has a home in Philippi and can provide for the needs of several others under her own roof. She is willing to share this wealth or offer it up to God. Lydia demonstrates one of the hallmarks of early Christian discipleship—radical hospitality. Her door is open. She provides food and lodging. She does not turn away the stranger in need. After Paul and Silas are miraculously released from prison, Lydia is there, once again, to provide for their needs and to take these missionaries into her home (Acts 16:40).

I can appreciate Lydia's readiness. After all, many times in my life doors have opened, but I have not been ready to act. Preparation and readiness are two very important ingredients to faith. Without them, we often miss opportunities to serve, to grow, to give.

The Christian faith is akin to the Boy Scout motto: Be prepared. Lydia is prepared. She is ready to act. She opens her bank account, her doors, her life whenever the need arises. Men, especially, would do well to approach faith with this same confidence and readiness. There are many opportunities that can pass us by—in business, in family, in the church. Being watchful is a first step in responding to God. Then we act.

 # She Said

When she and her household were baptized . . .

—Acts 16:15a

Lydia might offer modern disciples a model for integrating business and vocation with home and family. Too often we read books written by well-meaning experts in business on how to be effective, successful, and efficient in our corporate world, but very few business gurus ever ask the question, "How do we achieve, maintain, and balance effective, meaningful relationships with those in our house while our business is booming?"

Lydia was a single woman who owned her own business. She served as head of her household. She did not hesitate to execute her leadership within her home regarding the news of Jesus. She acted decisively and quickly and thus engaged her entire household in the faith of Jesus.

We know nothing more about Lydia's home or work life. How did she balance the responsibilities of her business with those of the people in her care at home? We have no information telling us if she was a single parent, widowed, or divorced. Did the household include children, servants, siblings, elderly parents, or relatives? The Bible is silent on all these issues. Nor do we know if she was balancing her work with caring for elderly parents who may have been sick or disabled.

I cannot tell you how many times I have heard the phrase, "Behind every successful man is a woman." This statement has served as a backhanded compliment to women for decades, but the comment does not resound today with all the changes occurring within gender roles. For example, what happens when the woman is the head of the household or is the primary breadwinner for the family? A neighbor of ours once joked that since she and her husband both had demanding careers, they both needed "a wife."

In American history, women began entering the work force in mass during World War II and have continued in business roles to the present time. Now both men and women must inquire about, and ponder how, to balance family and career while maintaining healthy vibrant relationships in all arenas. It seems that the old standard of "giving it all to your career" at the expense of family relationships is not as popular today as it once was.

Jesus calls us to serve all of those around us—whether it be our boss, secretary, coworker, mother, child, teenager, or aging parent. Jesus does not segregate, nor offer a hierarchy, regarding one being more important than another. His focus is different. Jesus said, "Who ever does the will of my Father in heaven is my brother and sister and mother" (Mt. 12:50). This is a challenge to us all.

DISCUSSION AND REFLECTION

1. Given what we know about Lydia's and Paul's personalities, what do you imagine their relationship to have been like?

2. Do you consider yourself a generous giver? Why or why not? If not, how can the church guide you into developing this quality of character?

3. How do you and/or your spouse balance work and home responsibilities? Who have been your effective and meaningful role models?

4. Share an experience when you were neither prepared nor ready to act on your faith. In retrospect, how would you approach the same situation today?

5. Discuss the differences between "belief defined as rules" and "belief defined as a relationship."

6. Where might God be calling you?

Chapter 12

Aquila and Priscilla

Acts 18:18–26

During the apostle Paul's so-called missionary journeys, he visited many cities and established many churches. Paul usually visited the local synagogue first and made his case for Jesus as Messiah. Usually, he was rebuffed. On some occasions, and at other times by attrition, Paul managed to find a few converts and usually an ample supply of helpers.

Among his more luminous assistants we find Silas, John Mark, and Timothy—who each either established or gave pastoral oversight to the churches Paul corresponded with. Aquila and Priscilla, a husband-and-wife pastoral team, pop up several times throughout Paul's letters, including his list of leaders in the Roman church (Rom. 16:3), his correspondence to the Corinthian church (1 Cor. 16:19) and in the pastoral epistle to Timothy (2 Tim. 4:19).

In each instance, Aquila and Priscilla are regarded as leaders of the church—most likely elders—their place in the early Christian movement is without peer. They seem to have been integral to the establishment of the church in Ephesus, where they opened their home (1 Cor. 16:19), rescued Paul (Rom. 16:3), and apparently served as copastors and teachers (Acts 18:18–26). They did, evidently, later return to Rome, where they became preeminent among those who were working for the gospel.

What do we know about them? What does this couple teach us?

Let's see!

 # He Said

After this Paul left Athens and went to Corinth. There he found a Jew named Aquila, a native of Pontus, who had recently come from Italy with his wife Priscilla, because Claudius had ordered all Jews to leave Rome. Paul went to see them, and, because he was of the same trade, he stayed with them, and they worked together—by trade they were tentmakers.

—Acts 18:1–3

The church—almost from the beginning—seemed to have difficulty living out the implications of the creed: "There is no longer Jew nor Greek, there is no longer slave or free, there is no longer male and female, for all of you are one in Christ Jesus" (Gal. 3:28). Rather, from the outset, Paul faced occasions where he had to address the peculiarities of congregations when it came to the roles of men and women or slave and free.

If Acts is truly a sneak peek into the very early church, it seems evident that men and women shared equally in leadership roles, while a strong ethic and pull to be counterculture marked the church's approaches to issues of slavery, eschewing personal property, and the value of human life (which was relatively cheap in first-century Roman-occupied territories).

Aquila and Priscilla, a Jewish couple accepted Jesus as Messiah. Their Jewish hospitality provided for Paul's needs, and their home later became a house church in Ephesus. Together, we assume they shared the leadership of the church, for where one is mentioned, so is the other. Evidently, coleading was not a problem in the early church—but it became so later. In time men and women were once again segregated to various roles in the church, and it's been something of a conundrum ever since.

Does God call only men to be pastors or leaders in the church? Aren't women called to share the good news, too—just as Mary Magdalene and Joanna did following the empty tomb? Why all this fuss about who has the authority to proclaim God's good news to others? Aquila and Priscilla may not answer these questions for us, but they certainly tell us that things were quite different in the early Christian movement. God was truly doing something new. God blew the old model out of the water. And today, are we still trying to get back to this Christian Eden?

 She Said

When Priscilla and Aquila heard him [Apollos], they invited him to their home and explained to him the way of God more adequately.

—Acts 18:26b (NIV)

Two of my first female role models of clergy were each married to a minister. Later, during my high school years, a variety of young couples would serve as my Sunday school teachers and as adult leaders for my youth group. In college, seminary and beyond, I interacted with even more couples who served Christ together through teaching, preaching, evangelism, social justice work, or missions. They all influenced and enhanced my understanding of the faith. These wives and their husbands showered many blessings on me. Their best gift to me may not have been correct teaching or profound advice, but their act of working side by side. Their teamwork and sense of purpose is reminiscent and reflective of another biblical couple.

Throughout Acts, 1 Corinthians, Romans, and 2 Timothy one special husband-and-wife team greatly influenced the ministry of the first-century church. These two, Priscilla and Aquila, model team ministry for us as they assist Paul, rescue him, teach, and host a house church together. This couple helped found three churches in Corinth, Ephesus, and Rome. Paul and Aquila clearly regarded Priscilla as an equal in church leadership and Christian education. Paul even calls her, as well as Aquila, a *synergos*, which means fellow worker. Today we might even consider Aquila and Priscilla one of the first clergy teams or missionary couples.

Likewise, a view of Christian marriage emerges as we glimpse the life and work of Priscilla and Aquila. This view is as fresh today as it was long ago. This couple held in common a much larger goal: the work of Christ and his church. This goal held them together during difficulty—such as the dark days when they were evicted from Rome because of their preaching. Certainly the foundation of their relationship was based on service—especially service lived out for others. This foundation gave their lives meaning and purpose. We never learn if Aquila and Priscilla had children or if they were not able to, but clearly the church became their offspring, receiving their undivided and devoted attention.

I am not advocating that every couple must be in full-time ministry to follow Priscilla and Aquila's example. I do believe that every marriage relationship, regardless of vocation, is an opportunity for meaningful Christian service.

Far too many of the biblical marriages we have explored in this discussion reveal disunity, disharmony, and discord between husbands and wives. What a delight to spend time with Priscilla and Aquila who seem to have gotten it right! Marriage is about much more than a couple's romantic love for one another. Marriage has an unexpected eternal impact. Challenged by the Sadducees on the topic of marriage in the kingdom, Jesus replied, "For when they rise from the dead, they neither marry nor are given in marriage, but are like angels in heaven" (Mark 12:25).

My own husband, not one to quote scripture very often, reminds me that when we get to heaven we will be brother and sister to one another. His reminder excellently reflects that our relationship needs to be about respect for one another as well as our intention to help one another grow in grace and service for Christ. In other words, marriage is about kingdom work.

 # He Said

Considering Aquila and Priscilla, I contemplate all of the couples who have influenced my faith. As a teenager, more than a few couples influenced my life—some in the church, some who were husbands and wives who coached, taught, or mentored. My parents, of course, were vital to me, but other couples came alongside me at various junctures to inform and inspire.

During my days in seminary I was still coming to grips with my call to preach. Jeff Davis and his wife, Marie, were instrumental in encouraging me in my stumbling attempts in the pulpit. Later, a younger married couple—Dan and Joy—modeled a form of shared ministry that was astounding and inspiring to many of us in divinity school. I think of these people now as I recall the shared ministry of Aquila and Priscilla, this pastoral couple who shared in Christ's work, who were itinerate, who sacrificed, and who truly lived in Christ. Priscilla and Aquila can serve as a model, I believe, for any married couple—clergy or lay alike—who desire to give more of themselves to Christ's work.

Something significant happens to us—to any marriage—when the partnership takes on a larger purpose. When a couple is praying together, serving together, giving together, and teaching together—whatever the roles—truly a new creation comes into being. That should be large enough for any marriage. It is exciting to see God's work unfolding when two people are living Christ's love for others.

 She Said

Paul went to see them, and because he was a tentmaker as they were, he stayed and worked with them.

—Acts 18:2b–3 (NIV)

America today would not be America without our addiction to sports. Our culture is inundated with sports images: from teaching metaphors, to coaching techniques, to leadership skills and teamwork analysis. Many of us spend our precious spare time with fantasy sports teams in fantasy leagues competing against fantasy opponents. One would think that with all this conversation and awareness of teamwork, people would know how to work on a team together. If your life experience is anything like mine, you probably agree that our society usually falls short when it comes to teamwork.

I have served a variety of churches—of different sizes and settings. During this same time period, four male pastors have either supervised me or were in a position as my senior pastor. Only in one church setting have I worked with a supervising or senior pastor who was female. I cannot say I was always a success in my ability to work on the same team as my supervising or senior pastors. Sin (i.e., personal woundedness, ego, ambition, or self-confidence) of mine or my colleagues often got in the way. We often talk a good game about being servant leaders, but in the pastoral office sometimes it is all hot air. Working together, letting go of egos, being supportive, and showing collegiality are often easier said than accomplished—whether in the office or the pulpit. I am sure these experiences would ring true in the classroom, the living room, and in the boardroom.

The unique relationship of Aquila and Priscilla, not only as a clergy couple, but in their rapport with Paul, can serve as a special blessing and a call to church leaders today. Here both genders model with one another how to work together effectively and efficiently. Harmony and unity replace friction and dissonance. We desperately need the witness of Priscilla, Aquila, and Paul today. Their collegiality as coworkers on Christ's behalf was perhaps their best gift to the early church. The strength that rose up from their united leadership, support, and collaboration with one another was the foundation of the church in their time. That harmonious strength, I believe, was their best legacy to us.

In 1 Corinthians 12, Paul gave us the image of the body of Christ to describe the functionality of the church. With that image he also provided what I like to call the "no compete clause":

"But God has arranged the body, giving greater honor to the inferior member, that there may be no dissension within the body, but the members may have the same care for one another" (1 Cor. 12:24b–25).

Here, I have to wonder who Paul had in his mind's eye as he wrote this passage. Was he thinking about his coworkers Priscilla and Aquila, who founded the church he was writing to? Did he bring their faces to his mind because he knew he needed them and their gifts as much as they needed him? Maybe Paul thought about their work as a team not just in stitching together tents, but their teamwork in weaving together a ragtag group of Jesus' followers called the church.

I believe that Paul realized that the work of God takes collaboration, cooperation, and encouragement because he had personally experienced that kind of rapport with Priscilla and Aquila. His ministerial life was his teacher. I pray that we may all learn from the example of Aquila and Priscilla because the work of God requires less of our bickering and power struggles and more of our harmony and collegiality.

Discussion and Reflection

1. Whether you are currently married or not, do you agree or disagree with the notion that Christian marriage is about service to one another and to others? Why or why not?

2. Share with the group other examples from your own life or history when both genders worked together as a team. What specific blessings have these role models given you in your working and/or living relationships with members of the opposite sex?

3. What are the blessings for the larger church when men and women colead or have opportunities to share in leadership?

4. Aquila and Priscilla obviously had a large leadership role in the early church. Why do you think they are largely ignored as models by the contemporary church?

5. Why do you think celibacy became the model for pastoral ministry in the church? How do Priscilla and Aquila model pastoral ministry?

6. Read 1 Corinthians 12:24–25. What does this passage say about working together in ministry? How have you seen this in the church today?